YOU KNOW
BTS?

First published in Great Britain in 2022 by
Michael O'Mara Books Limited
9 Lion Yard
Tremadoc Road
London SW4 7NQ

A CIP catalogue record for this book is available from the British Library.

Papers used by Michael O'Mara Books Limited are natural, recyclable products made from wood grown in sustainable forests. The manufacturing processes conform to the environmental regulations of the country of origin.

ISBN: 978-1-78929-415-6 in paperback print format

1 2 3 4 5 6 7 8 9 10

Designed and typeset by Claire Cater and Barbara Ward
Cover design by Natasha Le Coultre
Illustrations by Maurizio Campidelli
Decorative patterns from shutterstock.com
Cover photo: Axelle / Bauer-Griffin / FilmMagic / Getty Images

Printed and bound by CPI Group (UK) Ltd, Croydon, CR0 4YY

www.mombooks.com

YOU KNOW BTS?

BTS?

THE ULTIMATE
ARMY QUIZ BOOK
100% UNOFFICIAL

ADRIAN BESLEY

Michael O'Mara Books Limited

INTRODUCTION

In 2013, BTS made their debut in South Korea. They were seven young men fighting for a chance in the hyper-competitive world of K-pop. It wasn't easy, but they gradually earned a foothold in the South Korean pop scene and began to build an incredibly loyal following at home and in every continent around the world. They named their fans ARMY and together they went on a magnificent journey that saw BTS become the biggest band in the world.

Along the way, BTS have shown they are not just seven good-looking boys. They have spoken at the UN, campaigned on social issues, written and produced many of their own songs, and displayed astonishing talent in song, dance and performance. They have a great sense of fun, and each member brings something unique to the table. This book will test just how well you know every facet of the group.

ARMY are famous for devouring information about BTS, so any quiz book hoping to test their knowledge needs to delve deep. Though there are plenty of questions here that new fans will be able to answer, there are also many that will hopefully leave even the most ardent ARMY puzzled. Jin is famous for asking 'You know BTS?' – and you are about to find out if you really do . . .

QUESTIONS

DEBUT INTRODUCTIONS

1. My family name is Jeon and I am from Busan, South Korea. At 13, I auditioned for a talent show called *Superstar K* and after joining Big Hit Entertainment I was sent to Los Angeles for dance training. Who am I? ....

2. I was born in 1995. I spent less time as a trainee than any of the other BTS members – Big Hit suggested I took the stage name 'Baby G' but I declined. Who am I? ....

3. I only went to the audition in Daegu, South Korea to support a friend. I spent two years as a trainee before becoming the surprise member of the group, having been kept as a secret by Big Hit until debut. Who am I? ....

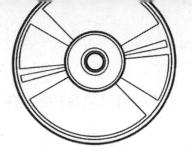

4. My older sister and I spent our childhood in Gwangju, South Korea. Before BTS, I was part of the underground dance team Neuron, and as a trainee I rapped on Jo Kwon's 'Animal'. Who am I? ....

5. I grew up in Ilsan, South Korea. At school I excelled in poetry and had an IQ measured at 148. I joined Big Hit in 2010 and, of all the members, I spent the longest time as a trainee. Who am I? ....

6. Born in 1992, I am the eldest member of the group. I was scouted for Big Hit while walking down the street. Before joining the company, I had no training in singing or dancing. Who am I? ....

7. I've been writing rap lyrics since I was a 13-year-old in Daegu, South Korea. I joined a hip-hop crew called D-Town before joining Big Hit as a music producer. Who am I? ....

THE ONLY MEMBER WHO . . .

1. Who is the only member of BTS who is ambidextrous?

    ....

2. Who is the only member who doesn't have pierced ears?

    ....

3. Who is the only member to have collaborated with K-pop legend
    PSY? ....

4. Who is the only member who is allergic to potatoes? ....

5. Who is the only member to have a secret handshake with Halsey?

    ....

6. Who is the only member who doesn't wear prescription glasses?

    ....

7. Who is the only member who wants to be a stone in their next life?

    ....

8. Who is the only member who doesn't have a driving licence?

....

9. Who is the only member who was Class President at school?

....

10. Who is the only member to have an 'ARMY' tattoo? ....

11. Who is the only member who has acted in a K-drama? ....

12. Who is the only member to have danced the *buchaechum* (a traditional Korean fan dance) on stage? ....

13. Who is the only member to have appeared on *King of Masked Singer*?

....

14. Who is the only member to have kept sugar gliders as pets? ....

15. Who is the only member with AB blood type? ....

16. Who is the only member whose mother has appeared on a BTS track?

....

ANIMALS

1. Which album were BTS promoting when they gave a BuzzFeed interview with puppies in their laps? ....

2. The video for 'IDOL' featured a tiger and a shark, but which animal appeared in the moon? ....

3. In episode 23 of *Run BTS*, each member was matched with a dog to perform tricks and agility. Which pairing won the competition?

    ....

4. And what breed of dog was Chopa – V's trusted hound in that episode? ....

5. In 2021, Jimin revealed he was allergic to which animals? ....

6. When Jungkook appeared in an episode of *Celebrity Bromance*, which K-pop star did he meet up with in a dog café in Seoul? ....

7. What was the name of the cat that befriended Jimin during their Summer Package in Hawaii in 2017? ....

8. In the official video for 'ON', what kind of animal takes a bite of Jungkook? ....

9. What kind of cat does Jimin refer to himself as? ....

10. What kind of animal was Jin convinced understood Korean during their Hawaiian Summer Package? ....

11. A frame-by-frame recreation of which BTS video performed by kittens has millions of views on YouTube? ....

12. What kind of animal did J-Hope famously say he hated? ....

13. In which country did Jimin meet Ziki the terrier puppy? ....

14. When did a onesie fashion catwalk reveal V as a kangaroo, Jin as a monkey, J-Hope as a rabbit, Jimin being a dragon – while Jungkook was a carrot? ....

15. And what animal onesies did Suga (appropriately) and RM (not very scarily) wear? ....

JIN BIAS

1. What kind of flowers is Jin associated with? ....

2. Who is Kim Butter Daddy? ....

3. At which winter sport does Jin particularly excel? ....

4. What name for Jin went viral following his arrival at the 2015 Melon Music Awards (MMAs)? ....

5. What did Jin persuade Big Hit to change their name (albeit briefly) to on Facebook in 2015 just because he was handsome?

    ....

6. What fruit costume did Jin wear in *BTS: House of ARMY*?

    ....

7. Prompted by V, what question did Jin ask Bang PD concerning their choreography? ....

8. In *Bon Voyage*, Jin approached strangers and asked, 'Do you know . . .' what? ....

9. Jin collects plushies and other merchandise of which animated and gaming character? ....

10. Where was Jin missing from at the 2020 Mnet Asian Music Awards (MAMAs)? ....

11. How did Jin appear on stage at the 2019 MMAs before his dance solo?

....

12. In which solo member's video does Jin bump into the main character before quarrelling with Jungkook in the background? ....

13. On celebrity survival show *Law of the Jungle*, what did Jin use as a fishing rod? ....

14. Jin supplied the theme and contributed to lyrics to which track on *BE*?

....

15. What kind of jokes is Jin renowned for telling? ....

SCHOOL TRILOGY ERA

1. In what month and year was BTS's debut single released (clue: Jungkook has a tattoo celebrating the date)? ....

2. Which song is about seeing photos of an ex-girlfriend on social media? ....

3. What was the first BTS single to break into the Top 100 in the Gaon charts in Korea? ....

4. Which member wore a mask – sometimes studded – through the promotion of 'No More Dream'? ....

5. What wardrobe malfunction befell Jin on their debut stage?

....

6. Who had orange hair for much of the *Skool Luv Affair* promotion?

....

7. Who drives the school bus in the 'No More Dream' video?

....

8. The 'King Kong' and 'shaving' were part of the choreography for which song? ....

9. Which rookie award did BTS not win: MAMA, MMA or Golden Disc Awards (GDAs)? ....

10. In a *Rookie King: Channel Bangtan* episode, what does Suga confess to stealing from Jungkook? ....

11. What colour outfits do the boys wear after the breakout of the schoolroom in the 'N.O' video? ....

12. Which song did BTS promote alongside 'N.O'? ....

13. Which song did Suga begin writing in his hospital bed?

....

14. In the Halloween dance practice for 'War of Hormone', V was the Joker and Suga was Chucky – but who was RM dressed as?

....

15. A remix of 'Danger' featured singer Thanh Bui – which country is he from? ....

PERSONALITY TYPES

1. Which two members of the group are Virgos?...

2. Which animal represents the Chinese zodiac sign of V and Jimin?

    ....

3. According to RM, which Hogwarts house do J-Hope and V belong to?

    ....

4. Into which Hogwarts house did RM place himself and Jin?.................

    ....

5. Which member of the group is a Sagittarius?...

6. Which member was previously an ESFJ but changed to INFJ in the
    2022 'MBTI Lab' video? ....

7. Which member was born in the Year of the Monkey?.........................

8. Which member is a Libra?..

9. Which member's MBTI type went from INFP (in 2017) to ISFP (in
    2020) to INTP (in 2022)? ....

10. Which member did RM decide would have been in Ravenclaw at Hogwarts? ....

11. Whose Myers-Briggs type changed from ENFJ to ESTP according to the 2022 'MBTI Lab' video (but they said they think they're actually ESTJ)? ....

12. What star sign is V? ....

13. Who retook his Myers-Briggs test in 2021 and went from an INFP to an ENFP (and remained an ENFP in 2022)? ....

14. Who among the members was born in the Year of the Rooster?

....

15. Which two members did RM decide were Slytherins?

....

MBTI: There are 16 MBTI types (e.g. ENFJ, ISFP), based on the Myers-Briggs theory of personality, and plenty of online questionnaires to find out which category you fit into.

NICKNAMES

1. What name did Jungkook give himself after rapping the words 'No true' on *American Hustle Life*? ....

2. Who is the 'Sunshine' of BTS? ....

3. What global title has Jin ironically bestowed on himself?

....

4. Which member might fans refer to as 'Joonie'? ....

5. The Korean pronunciation of J-Hope has led to which nickname?

....

6. Some ARMY have given which cute nickname to Suga as they think he has cat-like characteristics? ....

7. Which member might have been called 'Six' or 'Lex'? ....

8. Which nickname derives from the bird emblem of their home city and their love of a massive pop artist? ....

9. Jimin's soft cheeks led to fans giving him which Korean soft rice cake as a nickname? ....

10. In 2021, what special nickname meaning 'naïve and pure' did Suga reveal his father had given to Jungkook? ....

11. Who do ARMY know as BTS's 'God of Destruction'? ....

12. In the *Bon Voyage* trip to Hawaii, who named themselves 'Bread Genie', who chose 'Porrnesia Parrapio' and who declared they were 'J-Move'? ....

13. Which member has referred to themselves as 'Genius'? ....

14. V's love of a particular fashion brand has given him which nickname?

....

15. When asked what their English stage name would be, who replied, 'Christian Chim Chim'? ....

SUGA IN FOCUS

1. From which sport did Suga derive his name? ....

2. Which Suga-composed song won Best Soul/R&B Award at the MMAs on 2 December 2017? ....

3. What job did Suga do while he was a trainee to pay for his college tuition? ....

4. An injury to which part of his body caused Suga to take a break in November 2020? ....

5. What is Suga's real name? ....

6. What did Suga claim Big Hit CEO Bang Si-hyuk originally told him he wouldn't have to do as a BTS member? ....

7. In what year was Suga born? ....

8. On a TV show in 2016, Jimin revealed Suga had which 'cute' animal nickname when he was a child? ....

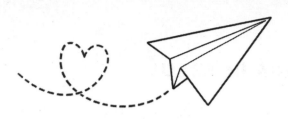

9. In 2021 Suga's remix of 'Over the Horizon' appeared as a ringtone for which phone? ....

10. Which solo track did Suga contribute to *Love Yourself: Answer*?

....

11. What was the theme of Suga's song 'The Last'? ....

12. Suga produced and featured on which 2020 song that reached No. 1 in South Korea and on the Billboard World Digital Song Sales chart?

....

13. For which personal idols did Suga produce 'Eternal Sunshine' in 2019? ....

14. Which song did Suga say he wrote when the group was considering disbanding? ....

15. Does Suga have a sister or brother and are they older or younger?

....

BTS VOCALS

1. Who is the group's baritone singer and is trusted to sing the lowest notes? ....

2. Who sings the first lines in 'Autumn Leaves'? ....

3. Which two members sing the bridge together on 'Fake Love' and 'IDOL'? ....

4. What vocal signature does Suga put on 'If I Ruled the World', 'Love Maze', 'Seesaw', 'Rain', 'Paradise' and 'Sea', among others?

    ....

5. A 2018 performance of which song on *Music Bank* saw the rap and vocal lines switch roles? ....

6. Jimin, Jin and Jungkook are all considered to have what kind of singing voice? ....

7. A performance of which cover song found RM harmonizing (rather well) with Jin? ....

8. Who joins Jimin to sing the outro to 'Life Goes On'?..........................

9. The music paper *NME* complimented Jin's chilling falsetto (sometimes called a scream) in the final section of which song?

    ....

10. To which song did Jungkook sing an a cappella part on *The Tonight Show Starring Jimmy Fallon?* ....

11. For which song does J-Hope have no lines at all in the studio version but usually sings RM's first verse in live performances? ....

12. Who sings the opening of 'ON'?...

13. For which song did Jungkook drop a 45-second alternative English bridge on Weverse in March 2021? ....

14. What improvised form of singing did Jungkook often employ during live renditions of 'House of Cards'? ....

15. Who provides the female voice on many BTS songs, including 'Spring Day', 'Love Maze', 'Magic Shop', 'Euphoria' and 'Moon'?

    ....

RM SOLO

1. Which of these names did RM not perform under before he joined Big Hit: Joon-dogg, Runch Randa or Largo? ....

2. RM's single 'P.D.D (Please Don't Die)' was a collaboration with which US rapper? ....

3. Which RM single appeared on the soundtrack for the *Fantastic Four* movie? ....

4. What was the name of the remix of Lil Nas X's 'Old Town Road' that featured RM? ....

5. The comeback trailer video 'Persona' finds RM in which setting?

   ....

6. RM's *mono.* mixtape features bittersweet songs about which two cities?

   ....

7. Which song on his *RM* mixtape is a specific retort to his haters?

   ....

8. J. Cole's 'God's Gift' provides the beat for which track on the *RM* mixtape? ....

9. The video for which *mono.* track features animated monochrome illustration by Choi Jae-hoon? ....

10. Which artist appears on 'badbye' on *mono.* and then featured RM on his own single in 2021? ....

11. Which song, released for the 2021 Festa, was inspired by one of RM's favourite pastimes? ....

12. Which 2017 song – a collaboration with Wale – addresses a failing education system, racism and cyberbullying? ....

13. Which solo track was written for 'those who prefer the night'?

....

14. Which collaboration with Korean singer Younha gave RM his first non-BTS No. 1 on the Billboard World Digital Song Sales chart?

....

15. RM featured on a remix of 'Champion' with which US rock band?

....

ALTERNATIVE JOBS

If the boys weren't in BTS, what would they be? They've given various answers over the years, but can you match each member to one of the illustrated clues below?

1. ....

2. ....

3. ....

4. ....

5. ....

6. ....

7. ....

BANGTAN BOMBS, PART 1

1. Which two members were the focus of the first-ever Bangtan Bomb?

   ....

2. In '95z Dance Time with a Beat App', which members team up to annoy their sleeping bandmates? ....

3. Who were the stars of the 'BTS' Vocal Duet "SOPE-ME" Stage' Bomb and what song did they sing? ....

   ....

4. Complete the title of this Bomb: 'Eyes, Nose, Lips . . .'

   ....

5. Where does the 'Runway in the Night' take place? ....

6. Which Bomb is the source of the legendary jibe 'Jimin, you got no jams'? ....

7. Jungkook sung a Trot (traditional Korean) version of which BTS song in a 2013 Bomb? ....

8. What was the name of the hilarious 2015 Bomb where BTS play a game in which they choreograph their reactions upon meeting each other?

....

9. What is the theme of the 2017 'GOGO Dance Practice (Halloween Ver.)' and who gets to play the lead character? ....

10. What was special about the Bomb that featured a 'Boy with Luv' dance practice in 2019? ....

11. To which song did BTS perform 'chair choreography' in a dance-practice Bomb in 2014? ....

12. Which dance cover did Jungkook and Jimin perform in a 2016 Bomb that has been viewed over 30 million times? ....

13. In the 2014 Bomb 'Nickname Tshirts! 95 cam #1' who were: 'Adult', '7th place in looks', 'I'm Not a 94er', 'Swag', 'Silly Hope', 'Power Blogger' and 'I'm a 97 Liner Oppa'? ....

....

14. In 'War of Hormone in Halloween', who is dressed as the Joker and who is Chucky? ....

15. What did Jin and Jimin dress as in '21st Century Girl Dance Practice (Halloween Ver.)'? ....

JUNGKOOK BIAS

1. Which 78-second-long demo did Jungkook release on his 22nd birthday? ....

2. Which eyebrow did Jungkook get pierced in 2021? ....

3. Which drink does Jungkook reportedly always have in his fridge?

   ....

4. What kind of wireless appliance is Jungkook said to collect?

   ....

5. Which member of GOT7 is a good friend of Jungkook's?

   ....

6. What does Jungkook's hand tattoo say? ....

7. Where on his body is the scar Jungkook received as a child after fighting with his brother? ....

8. What clothing trend was Jungkook said to have kickstarted when photographed at Gimpo International Airport in 2019?

   ....

9. Complete Jungkook's motto for life: 'It would be better to die than to . . .' ....

10. How did Jungkook treat the other members on his graduation in 2017? ....

11. Which Jungkook nickname began with a practice with RM backstage at KCon 2014? ....

12. What was Jungkook supposedly afraid of (in case they explode)?

....

13. Which single English word did RM teach Jungkook in his 'One-Minute English' video? ....

14. In the 2021 *Vanity Fair* video 'How Well Does BTS Know Each Other?', what did JK reveal as his favourite song to perform?

....

15. What did Jungkook do at BTS's performance of 'Airplane Pt. 2' at MAMA 2018 in Hong Kong to go viral? ....

....

ONLY ARMY KNOW . . .

1. How did RM translate V's thanks to ARMY for always giving them strength? ....

2. What word was coined for Jungkook's wide-eyed look of sheer confusion? ....

3. Who originally said 'infires' and what did he mean? ....

4. 'I know her face, but I don't know her name . . . I know movie, but I don't know movie name.' Who is struggling to name their Hollywood crush? ....

5. An old man's rasping pronunciation of which BTS member's name became an in-joke in the group? ....

6. What was J-Hope's reaction after his encounter with a boa constrictor at the zoo? ....

7. Fill in the gaps of BTS's *Bon Voyage* assumed name: 'International Pop-K Sensation ****** Rainbow ****** Transfer USB Hub ***** BTS'.

    ....

8. 'I'm Suga, ummmm, now I'm . . .' What is he now? ....

9. What polite English phrase did Jimin adopt during *American Hustle Life*? ....

10. What did J-Hope refer to as 'dirty water'? ....

11. What song do ARMY refer to as 'Queen' because of its enduring reign on the charts? ....

12. Complete the J-Hope exclamation: 'My heart is . . .' ....

13. Jimin and Jungkook's unruliness in an *Eat Jin* episode led to what famous command from the host? ....

14. Who has adopted the name 'bangwools' after an RM disclosure that they might have been called that? ....

15. Who are the Lamb Skewer Duo? ....

SHOW ME YOUR MOVES

Can you guess which song's choreography
each of these iconic dance moves comes from?

1. ....

2. ....

3. ....

4. ....

5. ....

WHO SINGS THE FIRST LINE?

1. 'DNA'

2. 'Blood Sweat & Tears'

3. 'Autumn Leaves'

4. 'Tomorrow'

5. 'Dynamite'

6. 'MIC Drop'

7. 'Jamais Vu'

8. 'Fire'

9. 'Dope'

10. 'Spring Day'

11. 'IDOL'

12. 'Attack on Bangtan'

13. 'ON'

14. 'Dionysus'

15. 'Fake Love'

WHO SAID WHAT?

1. 'I'm like a surfer, first you just paddle and fall off the board but as time goes by you can stand up on the bigger waves.' ....

2. 'I'll name my son "Kimchi is good".' ....

3. 'When something is delicious, it's zero calories.' ....

4. 'The next attempt may not be perfect, but the second is better than the first, and the third is even better than the second. That is the moment I decide, "I'm glad I chose not to give up." ' ....

5. 'Life is tough, and things don't always work out well, but we should be brave and go on with our lives.' ....

6. 'Regrets . . . revisiting what you didn't do well . . . it won't help you. The past is the past. Let's try to be a big person with a big heart.'

   ....

7. 'I have come to love myself for who I was, who I am, and who I hope to become.' ....

8. 'What is your name? Speak yourself!' ....

9. 'You are the most beautiful flower, more than anyone else in this world.'

....

10. 'Remember there is a person here in Korea, in the city of Seoul, who understands you.' ....

11. 'I want to be me, without too much decoration. I'm not one for showing off, so sticking out alone in the spotlight is not my thing.'

....

12. 'If you take music away from my life, there would be nothing left.'

....

13. 'We are always together. We know everything about each other, the good and the bad. These people who have made me who I am. Make me who I am today.' ....

14. 'The best moment in my life, from when I was born until I die, is seeing ARMY from the stage. And that will never change.'

....

15. 'Jungkook used to listen to me when he was younger.' ....

INFLUENCES

1. Which member lists A$AP Rocky, J. Cole, G-Dragon and Beenzino as role models? ....

2. Jimin and J-Hope both said the first albums they bought were by which Korean female solo artist? ....

3. At the Grammy Museum in 2018, the members chose their favourite genres. Who chose house and who picked jazz?

    ....

4. Which member said he started making music himself after hearing music by Epik High? ....

5. Who said: 'Kurt Cobain was my inspiration when I was a trainee'?

    ....

6. Which member said they auditioned for Big Hit after seeing a video of RM rapping? ....

7. Which K-pop pioneers' 25th anniversary did BTS celebrate with a cover version of their hit 'Come Back Home'? ....

8. Who did RM credit with showing him that a rapper could sing?

....

9. 'I was really impressed by her stage presence. She's a very small person and the volume of her singing and what she was able to do was very moving.' Who was Jungkook speaking about? ....

10. Which single-named solo artist (and now Hollywood actor) did V cite as a major influence when he started out? ....

11. Which member led the Wembley crowd in an 'Ay-Oh' Queen tribute chant? ....

12. Who chose John Legend as his role model and which member said Legend was his 'second role model'? ....

13. Which member is a self-confessed Belieber? ....

14. Which US R&B singer did Jimin cite as his biggest musical influence?

....

15. Which 'Kings of K-pop' boy group have BTS acknowledged as a big influence? ....

V BIAS

1. Which catchphrase derived from BBC comedy *Only Fools and Horses* did V adopt in 2021? ....

2. V's love of a certain designer brand led to him being called what kind of 'Boy'? ....

3. Which baby animals are often used to describe V? ....

4. Which nickname suggests V is so good-looking he must have been designed by a computer? ....

5. Which fruit did V once love but later say he wasn't so keen on?

....

6. What was V's neck tattoo image for the 'ON' 'Kinetic Manifesto Film: Come Prima' video? ....

7. V has three moles on his face: one under his right eye, one under his nose, and where else? ....

8. V's made-up phrase '*borahae*', conveying love and trust, literally translates to what in English? ....

9. V loves to imitate Brook, a character from which of his favourite manga series? ....

10. In which music video did V end up accidentally cutting his own hair?

....

11. *Burn The Stage* showed V having an argument with which member during the Wings Tour? ....

12. V is a long-time fan and friend of members of which girl group?

....

13. A September 2019 Bangtan Bomb saw V give a class in what skill?

....

14. Which 2016 variety show saw V pair up with actor and rapper Kim Min-jae? ....

15. V's 'dream came true' in a 2016 Bangtan Bomb – what was the dream? ....

ARMY

1. What does the acronym ARMY stand for? ....
    ....

2. Which BTS–ARMY event is the official celebration of the
    anniversary of the group's debut – Muster or Festa? ....

3. Which of these songs were not written for ARMY: '2! 3!', 'Go Go' or
    'We are Bulletproof: the Eternal'? ....

4. What name did BTS consider as an alternative to ARMY: 'Bell' or
    'Whistle'? ....

5. In what order do ARMY chant the members' names? ....
    ....
    ....

6. For ARMY's eighth anniversary, what kind of tracks were on the
    playlist that BTS gifted their fans? ....

7. When ARMY swept BTS to the Top Social Artist award at the 2017
    Billboard Music Awards (BBMAs), whose six-year winning streak did
    they end? ....

8. In what month and year was ARMY founded? ....

9. In June 2020, in just 24 hours ARMY matched BTS's $1 million donation to which campaign? ....

10. What was the name of Jimin's video which garnered the greatest number of views among the members' *Life Goes On* clips on BTS's TikTok channel? ....

11. Which special expression is the motto of ARMY? ....

12. What was the name of the 2021 ARMY Muster? ....

13. What is the name of the ARMY lightstick? ....

14. Which song did ARMY sing to BTS on the second night at Wembley Stadium in 2019 in a secret mission? ....

15. In 2019 ARMY created their own online awards show in opposition to which awards ceremony that had introduced an unnecessary K-pop category? ....

SPORT AND GAMES

1. In the 'Dynamite' music video, which member sings their verse on an outdoor basketball court? ....

2. In 2019, BTS were named official ambassadors for which decision-making game? ....

3. Which English Premier League football star loves BTS and said: 'I'm their biggest fan'? ....

4. In episode 5 of *In the Soop* season 1, whose baseball skills led to him being compared to *Twilight*'s Jasper Hale? ....

5. In 2017, BTS all donned baseball team shirts as Jungkook threw the first pitch at whose stadium in Japan? ....

6. In what famous London sporting arena did BTS play in 2019?

....

7. Which member is acknowledged as being BTS's football king?

....

8. Which three members of BTS are black belts in taekwondo?

....

9. Which former WWE wrestler announced he was a BTS fan back in 2018 and even offered to be their bodyguard? ....

10. In which event did BTS win three consecutive gold medals at the Idol Star Athletic Championships? ....

11. A 17-second clip on Twitter of Jungkook playing as Widowmaker went viral in 2019. Which video game was he playing? ....

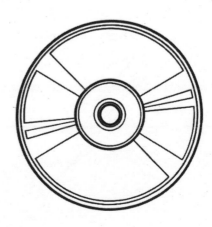

12. V, Jungkook and Jin were the BTS team who made the *ssireum* final at the 2016 Idol Star Athletic Championships. What is *ssireum*?

....

13. Which member dreamed of one day becoming a professional tennis player? ....

14. Korean team F1 and their stars Faker and Effort are big fans of BTS and played with the boys on a *Run BTS* episode. What game do they play? ....

15. At the MBC Music Festival on 31 December 2016, BTS performed a cover song called 'As I Told You'. What sport's clothing did they wear for the performance? ....

COMPLETE THE TITLE

1. '24/7= . . .' ....

2. 'Boyz with . . .' ....

3. 'Skit: One Night in . . .' ....

4. '21st Century . . .' ....

5. 'Best of . . .' ....

6. 'Jamais . . .' ....

7. 'Louder than . . .' ....

8. 'Fly to My . . .' ....

9. 'Blue & . . .' ....

10. 'Attack on . . .' ....

11. 'Spine . . .' ....

12. 'Inner . . .' ....

13. 'We are Bulletproof: the . . .' ....

14. 'The Truth . . .' ....

15. 'Go . . .' ....

ART AND LITERATURE

1. Which Hermann Hesse book was an inspiration for the concept of the *Wings* album? ....

2. Which image in the 'Spring Day' MV is based on the art installation *Personnes* by Christian Boltanski? ....

3. Which Haruki Murakami book is referenced in 'Butterfly'?

....

4. Which BTS member received a portrait of themselves from renowned Korean illustrator Lee.K as a birthday present in 2020?

....

5. The title character of *The Little Prince* by Antoine de Saint-Exupéry is the inspiration for which solo by a BTS member? ....

6. Which Van Gogh painting did V say he'd like to hang at home so he could look at it every day? ....

7. Which book by James R. Doty inspired one of the songs on *Love Yourself: Tear*? ....

8. Which German folk story provided the theme and title for a BTS song?

   ....

9. What pseudonym did V adopt out of admiration for the photographer Ante Badzim? ....

10. Which BTS video featured Pieter Bruegel's painting *The Fall of the Rebel Angels* and statues by Michelangelo and Cellini? ....

    ....

11. RM described seeing which artist's work at the National Gallery in London as a 'dream come true'? ....

12. Which BTS video alludes to Ursula K. Le Guin's story 'The Ones Who Walk Away from Omelas'? ....

13. *Map of the Soul: Persona* was inspired by Murray Stein's book on which philosopher? ....

14. Which book by J. D. Salinger – which appeared briefly in the 'Danger' MV – has been an influence on BTS? ....

15. The famous Manet painting *Le Déjeuner sur l'herbe* appears in which solo video? ....

SUGA BIAS

1. Back in 2010, Suga brought chicken to share with which member spending New Year's Eve on his own in the dorm? ....

2. On his 25th birthday, Suga fulfilled a promise to ARMY by donating what to 39 orphanages? ....

3. In the 2016 BTS Festa self-written profiles, Suga described himself as 'super . . .' what? ....

4. When he is not working or eating, Suga can often be found doing what? ....

5. What is Suga's favourite way to drink coffee? ....

6. Which BTS member accompanied Suga on a fishing trip during their 2018 hiatus? ....

7. When did Suga say: 'At the time it can be so hard and feel like the world is going to collapse, but after time's passed it becomes a time that you can think of with a smile'? ....
....

8. Which mischievous ninja character from a manga series did Suga dress as for the BTS V Live Halloween Party in 2015? ....

9. What was the name of Suga's female alter ego who appeared in a *Run BTS* skit in 2017? ....

10. Who or what replaced an injured Suga when BTS performed at the 2020 *SBS Gayo Daejeon* in Daegu? ....

11. What colour were J-Hope and Suga's original matching Sope tracksuits? ....

12. How much did Suga say his chain cost in his chat-up practice in *American Hustle Life*? ....

13. What kind of 'technology' did Suga use to describe his rap style?

....

14. At a fan event in 2014, a fan famously called Suga a 'dangerous man' and threatened to do what because of his sharp looks? ....

....

15. Suga has admitted to being a massive fan of which movie composer (whose soundtracks include the Pirates of the Caribbean series and the Dark Knight trilogy)? ....

GUESS THE SONG FROM THE WORD

1. Thyrsus...

2. Elton John...

3. New York..

4. John Woo..

5. Coca-Cola..

6. Nemo..

7. Bangtan Style..

8. King Kong...

9. Batman...

10. V App..

11. Kafka...

12. Epik High...

13. Jordan numbers.......................................

14. Usher...

15. Caramel Macchiato.................................

FEARS

Can you guess what each member of BTS is afraid of? There are a few red herrings in here just to make it extra-tricky . . .

1. RM ....

2. Jin ....

3. Suga ....

4. J-Hope ....

5. Jimin ....

6. V ....

7. Jungkook ....

A.

B.

C.

D.

E.

F.

G.

H.

I.

J.

K.

FESTA AND MUSTER

1. For their first Festa, BTS released a song looking back on the ups and downs of their first year. What was its title? ....

2. During Festa 2016, Suga lost at rock, paper, scissors and was made to take the dance break in which song? ....

3. For the 2017 Festa where members wrote their own résumés, who claimed to have international sports dance and *hotteok* (Korean pancake) making certificates and was competent in Word, Powerpoint and Cubase? ....

4. What were the group wearing for their Festa 2018 performance of 'Anpanman'? ....

5. Which now-fan-favourite song by the rap line was released for Festa 2018? ....

6. For the Family Portrait specials in Festa 2019 members were photographed in each other's solo sets. Which sets did J-Hope and Jungkook appear in? ....

7. What was special about the 2021 Family Portraits? ....

....

8. How long after their debut was the 1st Muster (this was a question actually asked at the 1st Muster!): 190 days, 290 days or 390 days?

....

Festa: Festa is an annual celebration of the group's debut which lasts around two weeks, leading up to the 13 June debut anniversary

Muster: Muster is an ARMY fan meeting / concert event that takes place annually, often during the Festa festivities

9. The 2nd Muster was called 'ZIP CODE: 22920'. Why that number? (Clue: it was originally called 'ZIP CODE: 17520' but was postponed due to the MERS virus outbreak.)

....

10. *House of Army* was a short film made for the 3rd Muster Zip+ with the boys playing a family of BTS fans. Who played the daughter and who was her mother? ....

11. What was the theme of the 2018 4th Muster, 'Happy Ever After'?

....

12. The 2019 5th Muster was named after which BTS song? ....

....

13. What happened during the performance of 'So What' at the 2021 Muster Sowoozoo? ....

14. Can you name both of the solo songs that the group as a whole performed at Muster Sowoozoo? ....

....

15. What does *sowoozoo* mean in English? ....

NAME THAT TOUR

1. South Korea, Chile, Brazil, USA, Indonesia, the Philippines, Hong Kong, Australia, Japan and Taiwan ....

2. USA, Brazil, UK, France and Japan

....

3. Korea, Japan, the Philippines, Singapore, Thailand, Taiwan – with extension to Malaysia, Australia and USA ....

....

4. South Korea, Japan – with extension to Taiwan, China, Japan, the Philippines and Thailand ....

5. Japan (× 4 cities) ....

6. Tour cancelled ....

7. South Korea, USA, Canada, USA, UK, the Netherlands, Germany, France, Japan, Taiwan, Japan, Hong Kong and Thailand ....

....

BEHIND THE SCENES

1. How is Kang Hyo-won, BTS's long-term producer, songwriter and music coach, better known? ....

2. Which producer and songwriter appears on 'Cypher Pt. 3: Killer' and on *Hope World*'s 'Hangsang'? ....

3. What kind of 'Noise' is the name of a Big Hit producer who has credits on 'Telepathy', 'Blue & Grey', 'Magic Shop', 'UGH!' and others?

    ....

4. Which BTS songwriter and producer, named after a small animal, became TXT's lead producer? ....

5. What name does the former singer J-Pearl, former member of boy group History, now BTS producer and frequent Suga-collaborator, go by? ....

6. What part do the Lumpens team (especially Choi Yong-seok) play in supporting BTS? ....

7. Ryujin made a notable appearance as J-Hope's love interest in the 'Love Yourself Highlights Reel'. Which girl group is she now a member of? ....

8. Former BTS backing dancer Lee Min-ho is now a member of which boy group? ....

9. Kim Jones designed the outfits for the Love Yourself: Speak Yourself World Tour. For which fashion house is he the artistic director?

....

10. What is the name of BTS's main manager, often spotted in paparazzi photos with the boys? ....

11. Who was the choreographer of 'Dope', 'Run', 'Fire', 'Blood Sweat & Tears' and 'DNA'? ....

12. Which long-time BTS producer and backing vocalist released her own debut single, 'Make U Dance', in 2021? ....

13. What is the name of the backing band that perform BTS's rock remixes live at concerts? ....

14. What role has Son Sung-deuk played for BTS since their debut?

....

15. Jessica Agombar co-wrote 'Dynamite' with which other songwriter?

....

'LA, LA, LA' AND 'NA, NA, NA'

Everyone knows that BTS love a good 'La, la, la' and 'Na, na, na' song, but how many can you name that have either of these combinations?

....

....

....

....

....

....

....

....

V IN FOCUS

1. What is V's real name? ....

2. In which city did he pass his audition to join Big Hit? ....

3. V has two siblings, but are they boys or girls and are they older or younger? ....

4. In what industry do V's parents work? ....

5. In which K-drama did V play the role of Seok Han-sung? ....
   ....

6. Is V the second oldest or second youngest in BTS? ....

7. V was a classmate of which member of BTS? ....

8. What is the name of V's friendship group with *Itaeowon Class* actor Park Seo-joon, actor and ZE:A singer Park Hyung-sik, *Parasite* star Choi Woo-shik and musician Peakboy? ....

9. Which iconic V line became a viral challenge on TikTok? ....

....

10. What do ARMY often call V – TaeTae, VeeVee or KimKim? ....

11. What instrument did V learn to play as a child? ....

12. What phrase does V often use in response to difficult times?

....

13. What colour was V's hair for much of the *Map of the Soul: Persona* era?

....

14. V made his runway debut in 2021 as a model for which brand?

....

15. What made RM dub V 'The Wind Prince'? ....

US AND UK TV APPEARANCES

1. When BTS appeared with Jimmy Fallon on *The Tonight Show*, which dance challenge did they take on with the host? ....

2. Which song did BTS perform on their appearance on *America's Got Talent*? ....

3. Which former boy band singer interviewed BTS on the BBC's *The One Show*? ....

4. On their appearance on *The Late Show with Stephen Colbert*, BTS (led by J-Hope) did an impromptu performance of which Beatles song? ....

5. Where was the venue for the *Good Morning America* Summer Concert Series that featured BTS in 2021? ....

6. What song did BTS perform a cover of on their visit to the BBC's *Live Lounge* in 2021? ....

7. In what year did BTS perform on US TV for the first time? ....

8. On which sitcom's TV reunion special did BTS make a much-hyped but brief appearance? ....

9. Who was the host of *Saturday Night Live* on BTS's 2019 appearance?

....

10. When BTS played 'Boy with Luv' on *The Late Show with Stephen Colbert*, their performance was a pastiche of which legendary group?

....

11. Which word did RM credit Ellen DeGeneres with introducing to Koreans after BTS's first appearance on her show? ....

12. Which member fell off the sofa at the fangirl prank on *The Ellen DeGeneres Show*? ....

13. What did BTS wear for their virtual performance of 'Life Goes On' on *Good Morning America* in November 2020? ....

14. Which iconic landmark was the setting for BTS's performance of 'ON' on *The Tonight Show* in February 2020? ....

15. Which member was absent from BTS's appearance on *The Graham Norton Show* in 2018? ....

INJURIES AND MISHAPS

1. Who remained seated, due to a calf injury, for the 2021 Permission to Dance on Stage concerts? ....

2. Where did Jimin's sparkly jacket get stuck during BTS's 2019 *New Year's Rockin' Eve* performance of 'Boy with Luv' in Times Square?

   ....

3. Who shed tears after a wardrobe malfunction during BTS's debut?

   ....

4. Jin reportedly had a bloody nose during the 2016 Idol Star Athletics Championships after an accident playing which sport? ....

5. What did Suga injure when he tripped on a door threshold in 2015?

   ....

6. In which country did RM have to avoid dancing at concerts in 2017 after stubbing his little toe? ....

7. In the final episode of *Burn The Stage*, Jimin is seen reduced to tears because he couldn't perform due to pain in which parts of his body?

....

8. Which member was, due to an injury, forced to sit on the side of the stage for BTS's first UK concert at London's O2 Arena? ....

9. Which member fell off stage after holding his breath in a game at a Japan Official Fan Meeting Undercover Mission in 2015? ....

10. Who led the group to fall domino-fashion in the filming of their 'Black Swan' performance for the 2020 *Gayo Daejeon*? ....

11. Suga wrote 'Just One Day' while in hospital with what condition?

....

12. What is thought to have caused Jin to clutch his ear in pain during a 2016 performance of 'Blood Sweat & Tears' at the One Asia Festival in Busan in 2016? ....

13. At MMA 2019, what caused Jimin to improvise while performing 'Dionysus'? ....

14. During a performance of which song on *Inkigayo* did RM accidentally rip Jungkook's shirt open wide? ....

15. Jungkook was seen to collapse with exhaustion in *Burn The Stage* episode 3 after a concert in which country? ....

THE MOVIES

ANSWERS ON PAGE 212

Can you match the favourite movie to the member?
There are two each.

1. RM: ....

2. Jin: ....

3. Suga: ....

4. J-Hope: ....

5. Jimin: ....

6. V: ....

7. Jungkook: ....

The Matrix, Inception, The Notebook,

Tazza: The High Rollers (2006 South Korean crime drama),

Born to Be Blue (the story of jazz legend Chet Baker),

Eternal Sunshine of the Spotless Mind, The Hangover, About Time, Southpaw,

Iron Man, Me Before You, Pretty Woman,

A Star is Born, 3 Idiots (Bollywood comedy-drama).

BANGTAN PETS

1. Which member's love of animals has led to fans giving him the nickname 'Gangyangi' – the Korean words for 'puppy' and 'cat' combined? ....

2. Which Jin solo track, released on SoundCloud, was dedicated to his pets? ....

3. What breed is J-Hope's dog Mickey? ....

4. V often calls his pomeranian 'Tannie', but what is his full name (meaning 'charcoal briquette')? ....

5. Which member named his family's spitz dog after himself? ....

6. Suga is sometimes called 'Holly's Dad' by ARMY. What breed of dog is Holly? ....

7. V's family look after his pet named Kkanji. What kind of animal is it?

....

8. Which member adopted their dog, who made a memorable appearance on the second season of *In the Soop*, from a shelter? ....

9. As a child, which member had a pitbull terrier and Korean jindo mix named Ddosun? ....

10. What kind of animal was Odeng? ....

11. Which is the bigger of V's older dogs, Soonshim or Ssyongssyong?

....

12. In a performance of which song on *Show! Music Core* in 2019, did J-Hope change the rap lyrics to include the name of BTS members' pets? ....

13. In *Bring the Soul*, which member drew a picture of his dog? ....

14. Jungkook's Maltese dog is named Gureum, but what nickname have ARMY given it? ....

15. Who shared the sad news of the death of his dog Jjanggu in 2017?

....

RM BIAS

1. What colour did RM dye his hair for 'Butter' – having said it would never be that colour again, as it reminded him of his 'dark side'?

   ....

2. In BTS's 2022 'Seasons Greetings' concept, was RM the Mystic Strategist, Shadow Hacker or Mad Scientist? ....

3. RM collects Pop Art vinyl figures by which artist? ....

4. In November 2021, why did RM claim on Weverse that he had just had the 'worst day' of the year? ....

5. RM appeared with a bandaged hand after suffering an injury while filming which MV? ....

6. Which sea creatures does RM famously love (but not to eat)?

   ....

7. What memorable hairstyle did RM sport at BTS's debut? ....

   ....

8. Complete the quote from RM's UN speech: 'Maybe I made a mistake yesterday, but yesterday's me . . .' ....

9. Which song from the Agust D mixtape *D-2* featured RM?

....

10. In what way is the number 148 associated with RM?........................

11. RM collects merchandise of which Kakao Friends character?

....

12. What colour did RM dye his hair for the promotion of 'Dynamite'?

....

13. With which *Harry Potter*-inspired exclamation has RM become associated? ....

14. In an episode of *Rookie King* RM had to dress up as which female anime character? ....

15. What general name does RM give to his leisure activities such as rambling, cycling and hanging out with friends? ....

AWARDS

1. BTS won their first award in 2013. Was it at the MMAs, GDAs or MAMAs? ....

2. Which song did BTS perform at the American Music Awards (AMAs) in November 2017? ....

3. Who did BTS present the R&B Album of the Year award to at the 2020 Grammys? ....

4. At the 2016 MAMAs, Jimin and J-Hope performed a blindfolded, synchronized dance to which song? ....

5. Whose photo of them with the band, taken after meeting BTS at the rehearsals for the 2020 Grammys, led to #WhereIsYoongi trending on Twitter? ....

6. When BTS won the Grand Prize award at the Asia Artist Awards 2018, which member claimed to have already forgotten the speech he had prepared that morning? ....

7. In what year did BTS earn their first *daesang* (Grand Prize)? ....

8. For which award show did BTS perform 'Dynamite' on the rooftop helipad of the Fairmont Ambassador Seoul hotel? ....

9. Who gave BTS their Sustainability Future Leaders Award for the third year in succession in 2021? ....

10. Which star did J-Hope pay homage to in the dance break of their 'Dynamite' performance at the MMAs in December 2020?

....

11. At the 2018 MAMAs, which member revealed that the group had considered disbanding during his acceptance speech for their Artist of the Year award? ....

12. Which future collaborator did BTS first meet backstage at the BBMAs in 2017? ....

13. For their red-carpet appearance at the 2021 Grammys, BTS all wore outfits from which fashion house? ....

14. What is the most *daesangs* BTS have won at a single MAMAs?

....

15. At the 2015 MAMAs, with which group did BTS have a dance battle? ....

WORDSEARCH

ANSWERS ON PAGE 213

There are 12 BTS songs hidden in the jumble of letters below. See how many of them you can pick out . . .

```
S K S K G N Z S X P D I D O L
A S H P Y O R E S P Y P T Q M
V K T J R C J Z K S N P L Z R
E E S P T I W N N O A D J B D
M U N M B M N K B V M P A A I
E P K X A A K G K F I T V Q O
B H G L D G S D E T E B F N
D O W I K B I R W A E Y W J Y
R R T H H R G C M Y Y K E Q S
R I E T L X V W S H X R B D U
J A N U O Q H Q S H Q C U A S
H Y W R N S B R O I O L T N O
M U N N L V F H Q N U P T G A
P I E D P I P E R G S T E E F
T N T G B L R L P M Z J R R V
```

BTS LIVE

1. In what kind of location did BTS perform live for their NPR Tiny Desk Concert in 2020? ....

2. What was the name of the 2014–15 tour that visited Asia, Australia, and North and South America? ....

3. In live shows, how have ARMY responded to RM when, in 'Reflection', he sings the line about how he wishes he could love himself? ....

4. Was the opening song on the first leg of the Love Yourself Tour: 'IDOL', 'Fake Love' or 'Dionysus'? ....

5. What was the final encore song on both nights of Map of the Soul ON:E? ....

6. What was the oldest song on the setlist of Permission to Dance on Stage: 'Anpanman', 'Fire' or 'Baepsae'? ....

7. In what song does J-Hope usually sing RM's first part in live performances? ....

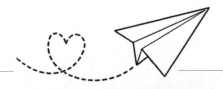

8. In which city did BTS perform songs from *The Most Beautiful Moment in Life Pt. 2* live on the day of release? ....

9. Which two members have played the piano during BTS shows?

....

10. At the KBS Song Festival in 2017 BTS played a rock version of which song? ....

11. Who wore a *Squid Game* costume at Permission to Dance on Stage?

....

12. During which song do Jin, Jungkook and V often imitate Jimin's moves as a prank? ....

13. In early concerts how did the group select a member to perform *aegyo* (acting cute)? ....

14. Which song was the focus of ARMY's Purple Ocean project where they covered light sticks with purple bags? ....

15. In live performances, in which song did V start his performance on an upright bed, dressed in silk pyjamas? ....

V SOLO

1. Which V solo appeared on BTS's 2016 album *Wings*? ....

2. Which solo track featured on the OST for Korean Drama *Our Beloved Summer*? ....

3. Where is V in the early morning in his solo song 'Scenery'?

   ....

4. To whom is 'Winter Bear' a tribute? ....

5. 'Sweet Night' featured on the soundtrack for which hit K-drama?

   ....

6. In April 2021 V released a snippet of an unreleased solo song on Twitter. What appeared to be the song's subject? ....

7. Which solo traces V's own journey from adolescence to adulthood?

   ....

8. What was the name of V's iconic solo V Live that was the first broadcast to surpass 500 million views on that platform? ....

   ....

9. Which 2020 song by V featured his friend and fellow Wooga Squad member Peakboy? ....

10. Where did V record the Bangton Bomb 'V's solo dance in the night'?

....

11. V said 'Winter Bear' was inspired by which 2013 British film?

....

12. What was the name given to V's solo dance step in 'Butter' when it became a viral phenomenon on TikTok? ....

13. The cover art of 'Scenery' is a photo of V doing what? ....

....

14. Which instrument did V play in his solo showcase on a 2019 Bangtan Bomb? ....

15. Which song on *BE* was originally intended for V's solo mixtape?

....

IN THE SOOP

1. Who spent their first afternoon in Chuncheon building a rubber-band-powered glider? ....

2. Why did Jin request a tank with flatfish at the house?........................

3. Which member do they deliberately pretend to leave behind when they set off back to Seoul mid-series? ....

4. Which song does V listen to when he is out on his own in the canoe?

    ....

5. What song do they compose while they are in the house?...................

    ....

6. Which pairing sing karaoke to Yoon Do-hyun's 'It Must Have Been Love' in the first series? ....

7. What board game do they play on their last night in Chuncheon?

    ....

8. Which pet accompanied the boys on series 2?....................................

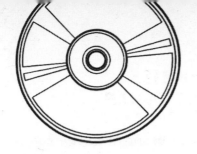

9. What instrument does V play by the pool?..

10. Which team won the foot volleyball match?..

11. What did RM name the moth that caused panic during dinner?

....

12. Who scares J-Hope when exploring the abandoned houses?

....

13. In which world did Jin spend hours during series 2?........................

....

14. What song's choreography does V perform during the poolside fireworks in the final episode of the second season? ....

15. What jobs were Jimin and V assigned in the discussion over BTS's planned DakgalBTS restaurant? ....

HOBBIES

The boys all have some interesting hobbies – can you guess whose is whose from the illustrated clues below?

1. ....

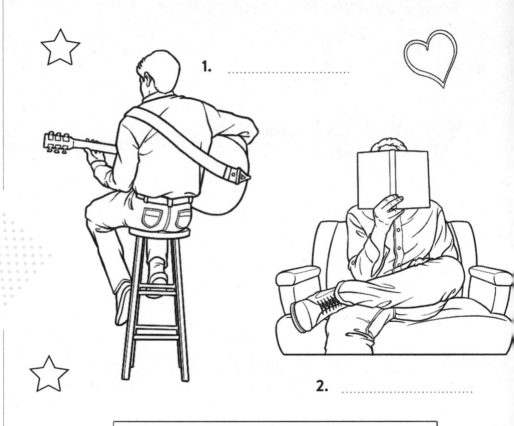

2. ....

3. ....

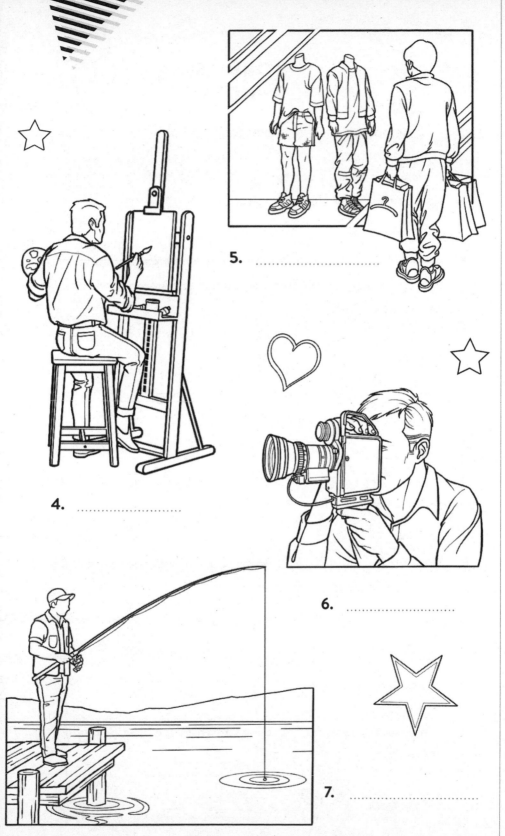

5. ....

4. ....

6. ....

7. ....

B-SIDES

1. Which Suga-penned ode to ARMY did BTS perform for the first time on their *MTV Unplugged* show? ....

2. What hidden track on *Love Yourself: Her* was originally titled 'Wherever there's hope there's a trial' (a quote from Haruki Murakami's *1Q84*)? ....

3. Which *Love Yourself: Tear* track was Jungkook confused about being asked to sing on V Live in 2021, before realising he only knew it by its Korean name, '*Nagwon*'? ....

4. Andrew 'Drew' Taggart co-wrote and co-produced 'Best of Me' – which EDM duo is he one half of? ....

5. Which track on *O!RUL8,2?* was written in response to the many criticisms BTS faced after their debut? ....

6. Which member co-produced 'Love Is Not Over' from *The Most Beautiful Moment in Life Pt. 1*? ....

7. What was the subject of 'Moving On' from *The Most Beautiful Moment in Life Pt. 1*? ....

8. What song from *BE* directly addresses the frustrations of the COVID-19 lockdown and quarantine? ....

9. Which angry track from *Map of the Soul: 7* has an exclamation as its (English) title? ....

10. Which B-side on *Wings* was BTS's first official fan song? ....

11. Which BTS title refers to the sensation of not remembering familiar situations or people? ....

12. Which song on *Love Yourself: Tear* is named after Pluto's asteroid number? ....

13. 'It's basically about life moving forward, no matter what happens, our lives go on,' said RM about which song from *Map of the Soul: 7*?

    ....

14. In the metaphor of 'Pied Piper', a track from *Love Yourself: Her*, who is the piper and who are the children? ....

15. What distinguishes 'Paldogangsan' (aka 'Satoori Rap') and 'Ma City' from other BTS songs? ....

B-side: Within K-pop, this refers to any track that isn't released as a title track/single

JIMIN BIAS

1. What special move does Jimin have in the 'No More Dream' choreography? ....

2. The video to which song led ARMY to call Jimin 'Little Prince'?

   ....

3. What kind of 'bug' do the BTS members claim Jimin has?..................

4. Which famous person wore a Chimmy onesie in a video wishing them good luck before their Citi Field Stadium concert? ....

5. When BTS performed 'IDOL' on the finale of *America's Got Talent*, Jimin went viral as 'the guy in . . .' what? ....

6. During a trip to the Philippines, which member had a nightmare and went to Jimin's room to sleep next to him? ....

7. What do the members mean when they tell someone 'You're Jimin today'? ....

8. What colour did Jimin dye his hair in May 2021 for their *Good Morning America* performance of 'Dynamite' and 'Butter'?

    ....

9. Which BTS song title is tattooed across Jimin's ribs? ....

10. What is the name of the friendship group containing Jimin, EXO's Kai, SHINee's Taemin, ex-Wanna One Ha Sung-woon and HOTSHOT's Timoteo? ....

11. In which video did Jimin wear a blue velvet jacket with a pink and black choker scarf? ....

12. At the 2019 MAMAs Jimin performed a no-hands cartwheel in which song? ....

13. Which gift from Jimin did V use as cover art for a solo song?

    ....

14. Jimin shared a dance stage at the 2016 KBS Song Festival with which K-pop star? ....

15. Jimin is known as BTS's 'Resident . . .' what? ....

YOU KNOW BTS MUSIC VIDEOS? PART 1

1. What basketball team vest does Jimin wear during the 'No More Dream' MV? ....

2. What word is spelt out on V's chain in 'N.O'? ....

3. What chore is Jimin doing at the beginning of 'Boy in Luv'?
    ....

4. What colour cardigans did the group all wear in the 'Just One Day' MV? ....

5. In 'Danger', while RM tries to write and Suga plays basketball, what does V do? ....

6. RM cuts a lonely figure in the 'I Need U' MV – where is he?
    ....

7. Jungkook stars in a giant teddy bear outfit in the 'For You' MV, but what kind of food are his leaflets promoting? ....

8. Which iconic band's logo does V sport on his shirt when underwater in 'Run'? ....

9. In the 'Fire' MV, what is written on the side of the car that falls from the sky? ....

10. In the 'Butter' MV, how many members are wearing black suits, and how many are in white suits? ....

11. What weapon does J-Hope wield in the 'Blood Sweat & Tears' MV?

....

12. In what language is the rent protest banner behind the boys dancing in 'Dope' written? ....

13. The Omelas building features in 'Spring Day' MV. Is it a café, a cinema or a motel? ....

14. Who is in the lead as the boys and their hooded asscoiates race across the wild expanse at the end of 'Not Today'? ....

15. What word is written on Jin's yellow jumper in red lettering in the 'DNA' MV? ....

SPOTIFY PLAYLISTS

In May 2021, each member unveiled a personal Spotify playlist. They've been updated since, but can you match a selection from the playlists as they were then to the correct member?

1. 'Up All Night' by Khalid; 'Work Out' by J. Cole; 'All I Want Is You (feat. J. Cole)' by Miguel; 'Goosebumps (Remix)' by Travis Scott; 'Astronaut in the Ocean' by Masked Wolf. ....

2. 'How I Move (feat. Lil Baby)' by Flipp Dinero; 'Walk Em Down (feat. Roddy Rich)' by NLE Choppa; 'Every Chance I Get (feat. Lil Baby and Lil Durk)' by DJ Khaled; 'Coco (feat. DaBaby)' by 24kGoldn.

   ....

3. 'Come Through (feat. Chris Brown)' by H.E.R.; 'Dive In' by Trey Songz; 'I Can't Be Myself (feat. Jaden)' by Justin Bieber; 'Wish You Would (feat. Quavo)' by Justin Bieber; 'So Sick' by the Star Cast.

   ....

4. 'Your Power' by Billie Eilish; 'Ashes' by Stellar; 'Hey Stupid I Love You' by JP Saxe; 'Peaches (feat. Daniel Caesar)' by Justin Bieber; 'Test Drive' by Ariana Grande. ....

5. 'Friends (feat. Party Next Door)' by dvsn; 'Self Care' by Mac Miller; 'Leave the Door Open' by Silk Sonic; 'At Your Best (You are Love)' by Aaliyah; 'Perth' by Bon Iver.

6. 'Grave Walker' by Dave Holland; 'Daisy Mae' by Raoul De Souza; 'Kora (Cornelius Remix)' by Go Go Penguin; 'Rio' by Florian Pellissier Quintet; 'Sometimes It Snows in April' by David Halliday.

7. 'Willow' by Taylor Swift; 'Iris' by the Goo Goo Dolls; 'Before You Go' by Lewis Capaldi; 'Adore You' by Harry Styles; 'Save Your Tears (with Ariana Grane)' by The Weeknd.

YOU KNOW BTS?

YOUTH ERA

1. What acronym is often used for 'The Most Beautiful Moment in Life'?

   ....

2. What professions did J-Hope and V dress up as in the 'Dope' MV?

   ....

3. In the 'Run' MV, whose hair was pink, whose was mint and whose was orange? ....

4. Which music video in this era was originally released in a version that was rated 19+? ....

5. 'Boyz with Fun' live performances featured a fun section where one member invents a dance move which the others must copy – which member set the challenge? ....

6. In spring 2015, the boys moved dorms. Which three members now shared a room? ....

7. In May 2015, BTS secured their first-ever music show trophy for 'I Need U' – but which one? ....

8. The members celebrated Jungkook's 18th birthday in a live broadcast. What did Jimin say he was going to give him as a gift?

....

9. In which song from this era do members use dialects from their respective hometowns? ....

10. What was 'The Butterfly Dream'? ....

11. Which song brings together the concepts of a lonely sea creature and an extraterrestrial being? ....

12. What was the theme of the concept photos for *The Most Beautiful Moment in Life: Young Forever*, shot on Jeju Island? ....

....

13. What enigmatic message ended the music video for 'Save Me'?

....

14. What alternative names are given to the track known in Korean as 'Baepsae'? ....

15. What was the group's first music video to surpass 100 million views on YouTube? ....

J-HOPE IN FOCUS

1. What is J-Hope's real name? ....

2. In what year was he born? ....

3. Complete the name J-Hope took as a young street dancer: 'Smile . . .'?

....

4. Is J-Hope from Seoul, Daegu or Gwangju? ....

5. For which entertainment company did J-Hope audition before he joined Big Hit? ....

6. Does J-Hope's father teach science, literature or maths? ....

7. What was the name of the underground dance team he was with before joining Big Hit? ....

8. In which sport did J-Hope excel as a young boy? ....

9. What kind of business does J-Hope's social-media-star sister, Jung Ji-woo, run? ....

10. Who is J-Hope's eternal roommate? ....

11. What brought J-Hope to tears on his first birthday after BTS's debut (2014)? ....

12. J-Hope is friendly with which member of Monsta X? ....

13. J-Hope fainted during the filming of which music video? ....

14. To which country did J-Hope go the first time he left South Korea?

....

15. Which weather-derived description is given to J-Hope on account of his positive and cheery nature? ....

CUT AND COLOUR

1. Who had pink hair in the 'I Need U' MV? ....

2. What colour hair did V have in the 'Boy with Luv' MV? ....

3. J-Hope wowed with which new colour at the Muster Sowoozoo in 2021? ....

4. *The Tonight Show* in September 2020 saw Jungkook sporting what new style? ....

5. Who surprised ARMY with green highlights and full bangs for the 'Run' MV? ....

6. What MV witnessed Jimin's iconic rainbow hair? ....

7. What iconic look did Suga take on as the king in the 'Daechwita' MV?

   ....

8. On which tour did Jin reveal his much-loved purple hair?........................

9. Whose style in the 'Permission to Dance' MV was described as 'emo'?

....

10. Just before BTS appeared at 5th Muster Magic Shop in Osaka, Japan in 2019, Jimin debuted which new hair colour in a Twitter selfie? ....

11. Which member sported bright yellow hair in the 'Butter' MV?

....

12. At which award show in 2021 did Suga appear on the red carpet with orange locks? ....

13. What feature of Jin's hairstyles always sends shockwaves through Twitter? ....

14. The release of which MV saw the name 'bluejoon' go viral?

....

15. What was notable about the members' hair in an ad for LG in 2018?

....

WHO SAID WHAT ABOUT WHOM?

1. '[He] winds me up all the time but never stops smiling even when he does that. But you can never punch someone who looks so happy like that.' ....

2. 'He has this innocence in him that makes him lovable – he is loved by so many. And I think that trait also enabled us to become best friends.' ....

3. 'He looks so big like a giant. He's the *hyung* that makes me feel immensely proud.' ....

4. 'You told me this a month ago that your black underwear is missing. Sorry, that was me.' ....

5. 'His answers are always the same, so I don't feel like I'm complimenting him anymore.' ....

6. 'When I'm in the bathroom to cry, you still cry with me. And you come see me at dawn to laugh alongside me. You care about me and have me in your thoughts.' ....

7. 'We talked about how we can lead the "kids", take good care of them, and become a better group.' ....

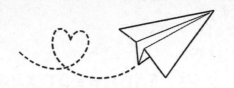

8. '[He] has his own energy. He doesn't like a depressing atmosphere, so I think he always brings energy into the team.' ....
....

9. 'He worries a lot and he's vulnerable to flattery.' ....
....

10. 'We're very close, but there's a little bit that's complicated and awkward.' ....

11. 'He's good at "turning off" my bad habits. He's really sociable so he's good at mixing with others.' ....

12. 'I've been raising *hyung* up from when I was 15 years old until now.'
....

13. 'He knows a lot about different things and he uses that to always help people. It's so funny how he gets all this random information.'
....

14. 'In the effort squad, he's the triple-A *hyung*, and he's timid but shameless and hates to lose.' ....

15. 'Honestly, he's the same as me. Hopeless.' ....

JUNGKOOK SOLO

1. 'Nothing Like Us', 'Purpose' and '2U' were among Jungkook's covers that were originally recorded by which artist? ....

2. Which Jungkook self-produced ballad broke SoundCloud's 'most commented' and 'most liked' records in the first 24 hours? ....
   ....

3. Which cover did Jungkook upload two years to the day after BTS's last concert before lockdown? ....

4. Where was Jungkook when he recorded the version of Lauv's 'Never Not' that he posted on Twitter in May 2020? ....

5. Which 2022 Jungkook solo was produced and co-written by Suga for the *7Fates: Chakho* webtoon? ....

6. Which solo saw Jungkook literally take flight on the Speak Yourself Tour? ....

7. What was notable about what Jungkook did with IU's 'Ending Scene' on SoundCloud in January 2019? ....

8. Which member of BTS encourages Jungkook and plays the instrumental when he sings Tori Kelly's 'Dear No One'? ....

9. Which Tori Kelly cover did Jungkook upload to BTS's SoundCloud account on Christmas Day 2015? ....

10. How many hours were in the title of the Dan + Shay and Justin Bieber cover that Jungkook tweeted and deleted in 2020? ....

11. Jungkook celebrated the 2018 White Day (when Korean men give gifts to women) by posting which Roy Kim cover on Twitter, which he captioned 'Song for ARMY'? ....

12. Jungkook recorded Adam Levine's 'Lost Stars' for SoundCloud in 2015 but where did ARMY see him perform the song to his bandmates and a small crowd? ....

13. Which 'Lady' duetted with Jungkook, singing 'I'm In Love' on *The Masked Singer* in 2016? ....

14. Which is Jungkook's solo song from the *Wings* album? ....

15. In January 2020 Jungkook dropped a cover of the 1989 song 'Perhaps That Was Love' by Choi Yong-joon. On Weverse who did he pick out as liking that song? ....

BANGTAN UNIVERSE

1. In which fictional South Korean city does the fictional parallel Bangtan Universe (BU) mainly take place? ....

2. What word does Taehyung carve into the shop shutter? ....

3. Where was Hoseok abandoned by his mother as a young boy?

   ....

4. What is the name of the fictional flower that is a constant symbol in BU? ....

5. To which country does Seokjin go when he leaves the school in Korea?

   ....

6. Which character lives in a container house in BU? ....

7. Who does Taehyung murder in BU? ....

8. What do you exchange for a 'positive attitude' at the Magic Shop?

   ....

9. Throughout the story Namjoon is shown to have a special bond with which character? ....

10. What does Hoseok exchange for cake at the Magic Shop? ....

....

11. Who is the only character who does not appear to have a tragic back story in BU? ....

12. Where is Yoongi when he starts the fire? ....

13. Which character appears in a wheelchair in the 'Love Yourself Highlight Reel'? ....

14. Which of these music videos does not include BU content: 'Run', 'ON' or 'Fake Love'? ....

15. What kind of animal gives Seokjin a message when he realizes he can time-travel? ....

BU: The BU (Bangtan Universe) is a fictional parallel reality and is the setting for a story revealed through music videos, short films, books and other BTS content through the years. It is a complex narrative that jumps back and forth across time and leaves fans to decode, analyse and come up with their own theories about what happens and what it all means.

YOU KNOW BTS?

ICONIC MUSIC VIDEO MOMENTS

Each of the illustrations below represents something that appears in a BTS music video – can you name the songs?

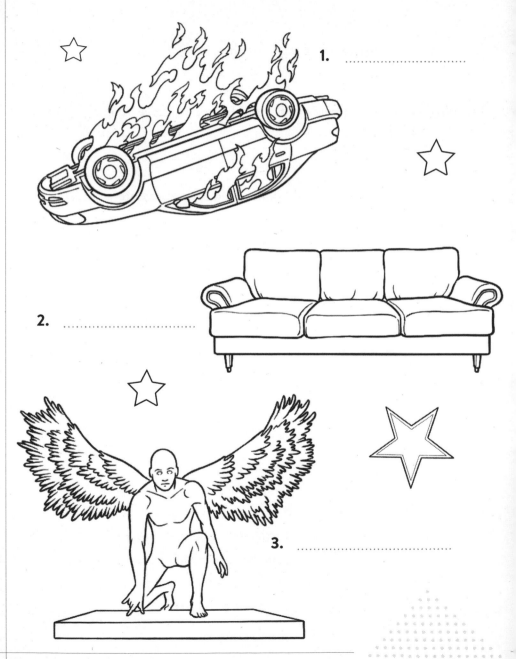

1. ....

2. ....

3. ....

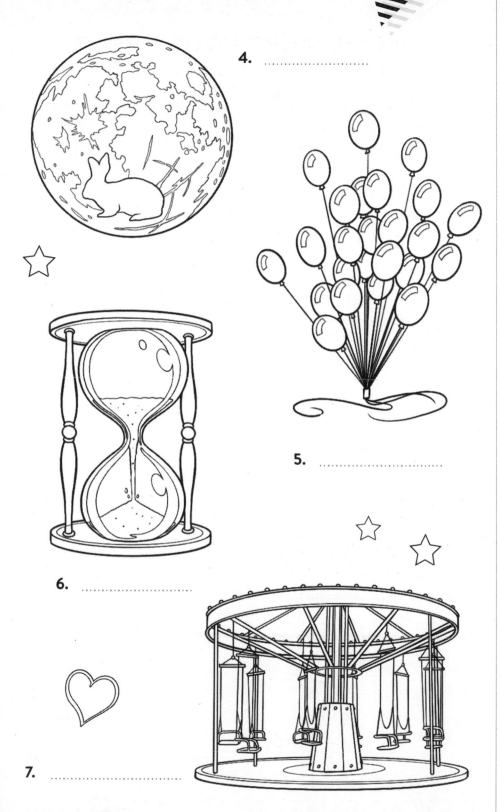

4. ....

5. ....

6. ....

7. ....

BTS ON *THE LATE LATE SHOW WITH JAMES CORDEN*

1. What was Jin's response when Corden claimed he too was nicknamed 'Worldwide Handsome' as a schoolboy? ....

2. Which Post Malone song did the group sing along to on their Carpool Karaoke drive? ....

3. What is ARMY's Jimin-associated nickname for James Corden?

   ....

4. Which celebrity joined Corden to search for the boys in the game of hide-and-seek? ....

5. Which member was the last to be caught in the game? ....

6. On the 2020 show, what did Suga tell James he wanted BTS to get at the next Grammys? ....

7. What game – where James fires fruit at them as they stand behind a plexiglass wall – did BTS play on their first appearance on *The Late Late Show*? ....

8. The 'Life Goes On' performance on *The Late Late Show* begins with Jungkook reading from a newspaper. What is the paper's headline?

....

9. The 'Dynamite' performance on *The Late Late Show* ended in a chat-show set – which member took the role as host? ....

10. What song did BTS perform when they appeared remotely on the 'Homefest' COVID-19 lockdown version of *The Late Late Show?*

....

11. What activity did the group join James Corden in during the Carpool Karaoke segment: basketball, dance class or busking? ....

12. Which song was performed live on TV for the first time on *The Late Late Show* in 2020? ....

13. Which song did BTS perform in the middle of the street for the 'Crosswalk Concert' segment of the 2021 show? ....

14. American news anchor Cher Calvin went on Instagram to show which member's fingerprints after he touched her car during the 'Crosswalk Concert' on the 2021 show? ....

15. 'You're in some *** ***** with ARMY,' said RM to Corden on the 2021 show. Can you fill in the missing words? ....

WORLD RECORDS

1. BTS won a record number of awards at the Japan Gold Disc Awards in 2021. How many did they take home? ....

2. BTS broke the Guinness World Record for most viewers of a music concert livestream twice in one year. With which concerts?

   ....

3. In September 2021, Jungkook became the first person to have how many tweets that had been retweeted over a million times? ....

4. In July 2021, when 'Permission to Dance' went to No. 1 on the Billboard Hot 100, they achieved which feat, last accomplished by Drake in 2018? ....

5. In December 2020, BTS became the first artist ever to win how many music shows in one year in South Korea – 30, 40 or 50?

   ....

6. In 2021, BTS became the first artist ever to top Billboard's World Digital Song Sales chart with 31 different songs. What 5-year-old solo track was the 31st? ....

7. In which year did BTS become the first artists to sweep the MMA and MAMA *daesangs* in the same year? ....

8. In 2020, what became the fastest music video by a Korean soloist to reach 4 million likes on YouTube? ....

9. BTS set the record for the fastest time to reach 1 million followers on TikTok – how many hours (plus 31 minutes) did it take them? ....

10. In 2019, which member set a new record as the only artist ever to achieve the Top 20 All Kill on Twitter worldwide trends? ....

11. Whose 36-year-long record of being the only international act to top the Japanese Oricon Music Chart did BTS beat in 2020? ....

....

12. Which single gave them their first Billboard No. 1, making them the first all-South Korean act to earn a No. 1 single in the United States?

....

13. Whose single topped the iTunes chart in 117 countries, breaking Adele's record as the soloist with the most iTunes No. 1s? ....

14. Who was the first Korean solo artist to reach 7.5 million followers on Spotify? ....

15. To the nearest million, how many people simultaneously watched the premiere of 'Butter' on YouTube? ....

MAP OF THE SOUL ERA

1. Which two fruits featured in the elegant Version 4 concept photos for *Map of the Soul: Persona*? ....

2. Which song from *Map of the Soul: Persona* was used as the closing song throughout their 2019 Speak Yourself Tour? ....

3. 'Home' mirrors lines from which earlier BTS song? ....

4. Which member was nicknamed 'the Human Grapefruit' early in this era? ....

5. Which member wielded a staff, or *thyrsus*, during live performances of 'Dionysus'? ....

6. 'Make It Right' collaborator Lauv first met the group backstage after a concert in which city? ....

7. For approximately how many weeks did BTS take an extended break in summer 2019? ....

8. What was the name of BTS's global art project, which launched in January 2020? ....

9. J-Hope's lamp-post dance in the 'Boy with Luv' video is a homage to a scene from which classic Hollywood movie? ....

10. Where did BTS's free mini-show for the *Good Morning America* Summer Concert take place in May 2019? ....

11. Which track from *Map of the Soul: 7* had an 'art film' video featuring an interpretive dance performance to an orchestral version of the song? ....

12. Which female singer featured on a remix of 'ON'? ....

13. At which iconic landmark did BTS perform 'ON' for *The Tonight Show?* ....

14. Which track on *Map of the Soul: 7* is performed by the four members of the vocal line? ....

15. Which video produced for Festa 2020 portrayed the group's journey as an animation? ....

JIN IN FOCUS

1. What is Jin's birth name? ....

2. In what year was Jin born? ....

3. How many siblings does Jin have? ....

4. What was Jin's reaction when first approached by Big Hit talent scouts in the street? ....

5. Jin is in the 'We're the Best Idol' club with a few other K-pop stars – what do they do? ....

6. Who has been known as Jin's 'Eternal Roommate' since they first shared a bedroom in 2015? ....

7. In 2018, Jin and his brother opened a restaurant serving what kind of food? ....

8. In what country did Jin live for a short period as a middle-school exchange student? ....

9. What is the name of Jin's occasional *mukbang* (eating) V Lives where he eats food while chatting to ARMY? ....

10. Who gave Jin the name 'Worldwide Handsome'? ....

11. Jin was appointed a Character Design Judge for which of his favourite video games? ....

12. What outdoor activity does Jin enjoy, often persuading Suga to do with him? ....

13. What surprise would Jin regularly reveal on stage during the Wings Tour? ....

14. What song did Jin sing with V for the *Hwarang: The Poet Warrior Youth* original soundtrack? ....

15. What number 'guy from the left' went viral when Jin was photographed with the group at the 2017 BBMAs? ....

BTS ON THE BIG SCREEN

1. In *Burn The Stage*, what did Jungkook beg Yeontan not to do?

    ....

2. What mushroom-lookalike did Jungkook slip into Jin's ramyeon in *Burn The Stage?* ....

3. What kind of party do the group enjoy in LA in *Burn The Stage?*

    ....

4. During *Burn The Stage*, we hear how J-Hope and Jungkook once argued over what insignificant thing? ....

5. In which city did the rooftop conversation between members in *Bring The Soul* take place? ....

6. Which song do they break into at the K-BBQ restaurant in LA during *Bring The Soul?* ....

7. Which museum does BTS visit and conduct an interview in during *Bring The Soul?* ....

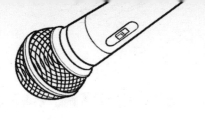

8. Which *D-2* track did Suga reveal the beat for in *Bring The Soul*, naming it 'Chile, I'm Hungry'? ....

9. Also in this section, who does Suga say he is often mistaken for – to V's outraged surprise? ....

10. Can you complete the tagline that accompanied *Break The Silence* promotions: 'Facing my other self . . .'? ....

11. The first scene of *Break The Silence* finds the boys on a hotel rooftop in which city? ....

12. What kind of gallery did RM visit in *Break The Silence*? ....

13. In *Break The Silence*, which member questions his own talent and feels he needs to work harder to match the others? ....

14. In the *Bring The Soul* after-credits Jungkook (ironically) says he's sure fans will want to see how he does what? ....

15. What didn't Suga do during live perfomances that made the members tease him in *Break The Silence*? ....

JAPAN, PART 1

1. In the music video for 'Lights', who is the last to take their seat in the cinema?

2. Which 2018 song was chosen as the new theme for the Japanese love reality show *The Moon and the Wolves* in 2020?

3. Which BTS release in 2018 was replaced by a Japanese version of 'Airplane Pt. 2' and 'Fake Love' after protests in Korea against the lyricist, Yasushi Akimoto?

4. 'Don't Leave Me' was BTS's first Japanese Drama OST. For which police series was it written?

5. What was the title of BTS's first song to appear originally in Japanese?

6. When was BTS's Japanese debut: July 2013, December 2013 or June 2014?

7. In what outfits did BTS dance to 'Spring Day' at the 2018 4th Muster in Japan?

8. Which Japanese hip-hop artist translated and wrote lyrics for many of BTS's Japanese hits? ....

9. In which city was BTS's first Asian concert outside Korea (part of the Red Bullet Tour)? ....

10. What was the name of BTS's first Japanese album? ....

11. What are BTS called in Japan? ....

12. Can you complete the name of BTS first Japanese concert tour in 2015: Wake Up: . . .? ....

13. 'Film Out' was the first single from which album? ....

14. Their Japanese track 'Pt. 2 In That Place' was an answer to which earlier BTS song? ....

15. Which iconic rap label manages BTS in Japan? ....

SUGA SOLO

1. What alias did Suga assume for his solo mixtapes and why did he choose that name? ....

2. What was Suga's 'First Love' according to his solo on the *Wings* album? ....

3. Which solo track from *Love Yourself: Answer* features Suga singing?

   ....

4. Who does Suga rap with on his *D-2* song 'Strange'?.....................

5. Lines from which *D-2* diss track were originally part of 'BTS Cypher Pt. 4'? ....

6. Which Suga track appears on Halsey's 2020 album *Manic*?

   ....

7. Suga featured on 'Blueberry Eyes', repaying a favour to which singer who joined him on *D-2*'s 'Burn It'? ....

8. In which of his solo songs does Suga recall the bittersweet feeling of finishing each gruelling day? ....

9. Which Agust D song is linked to the 1983 movie *Scarface*?

....

10. 'Intro: Dt sugA' and 'Agust D' both sample which James Brown track?

....

11. Who dies at the end of the 'Daechwita' MV?...............................

12. Suga featured on which single by Lee So-ra in 2019?.....................

13. According to the first line of 'Interlude: Shadow', what does Suga want to be? ....

14. Which *D-2* track tells of a childhood friend who took a different path to Suga? ....

15. What did Suga hold during the performance of 'Daechwita' at Muster Sowoozoo in 2021? ....

COVER VERSIONS

1. Which cover of a Seo Taiji & Boys song was part of that group's 25th-anniversary album project in 2017? ....

2. In their 2021 *MTV Unplugged Presents* stage, BTS performed which massive 2005 hit? ....

3. In 2017, Jimin and Jungkook covered 'We Don't Talk Anymore'. Who sang Charlie Puth's part and who sang Selena Gomez's? ....

    ....

4. BTS's performance of an 8Eight song at the 2017 GDAs is an ARMY favourite. What is the title of that song? ....

    ....

5. V and Jungkook covered songs by which K-pop group when they appeared on Mnet's 'Burning Karaoke' in 2016? ....

6. What was the name of BTS's version of a track of a similar title by American rapper J. Cole? ....

7. Who accompanied Jungkook on a V Live broadcast in a rendition of Hwang Chi-yeul's 'A Daily Song'? ....

8. On their BBC Live Lounge appearance, BTS covered which 1997 Faith Evans and Puff Daddy hit? ....

9. Just six months after their debut, four members of BTS made a music video covering which Mariah Carey song? ....

10. Which Christmas song was covered by Jimin and RM in 2019 and BTS (minus an injured Suga) in 2020? ....

11. On New Year's Eve in 2015, during the MBC Music Festival, BTS covered which Shinhwa song? ....

12. Jungkook's cover of 'Falling' appeared on YouTube in 2021. Who recorded the original? ....

13. Which member joined up with Jungkook in 2015 to record a cover of Troye Sivan's 'Fool'? ....

14. Which Harry Styles song did BTS sing the refrain of together on various chat shows in 2020? ....

15. For the 2016 MBC *Gayo Daejejeon*, Jungkook, with BTS members (except injured Suga) as backing dancers, performed which Rain hit?

....

JET-SETTING

1. What did Jimin lose shortly after he landed in Bergen, Norway?

   ....

2. Jungkook and Jimin drove off leaving J-Hope where in New Zealand?

   ....

3. Who sang Lee Hyun's '30 Minutes Ago' in the New Zealand 'caraoke'? ....

4. The 2018 Summer Package in Saipan saw the boys trying to remember the blanks in their what? ....

5. What sport did Jin and Jimin try in their 2016 Summer Package in Dubai? ....

6. Where did BTS go for their first Winter Package, released in January 2020? ....

7. What did Suga, Jimin and Jungkook make while the others went to the zipwire in the 2021 Winter Package? ....

8. What did Team B (including a petrified Jin) have to kiss to get to ride the Jetovator in Valletta, Malta? ....

9. What did V and Jimin write in the snow in New Zealand? ....

10. Whose heartfelt letter to whom in Hawaii ended with a PS asking them to act their age? ....

11. Which members entered the frozen lake after the games in the sauna in Finland? ....

12. V gave a short performance on the streets of Valletta, Malta, of which song? ....

13. What game did they play after dinner on the last night in New Zealand that left Suga owing everyone a meal? ....

14. V had henna tattoos of what drawn on his ankles in Gozo, near Malta?

    ....

15. BTS's 2019 Summer Package took place in Wanju – in which country? ....

JIMIN IN FOCUS

1. Which song was Jimin dancing to in the first solo-focus fancam to reach 100 million YouTube views in K-pop history? ....

2. Which subject did Jimin study and excel in at Busan High School of Arts before joining Big Hit? ....

3. What number does Jimin have tattooed on his wrist? ....

4. What is the name of the Busan café run by Jimin's father?

    ....

5. Jungkook likes to tease Jimin about which characteristic?

    ....

6. What is Jimin's birth name? ....

7. Is Jimin known as an optimist, a perfectionist or a pessimist? ....

    ....

ANSWERS ON PAGE 216

8. What nickname was Jimin given at school as he looked like a puppy?

....

9. Why did Jimin cry in the final episode of *Burn The Stage?* ....

....

10. What name is given to Jimin for his ability to draw in new fans?

....

11. What colour is Jimin's hair in the 'Spring Day' music video?

....

12. Which member once said he would like Jimin to date his sister?

....

13. Jimin and which member shared a room for the longest?

....

14. Jimin trained for ten years in which sport before becoming a dancer?

....

15. Jimin has a scar from a childhood accident. Where on his body?

....

COVER ART AND CONCEPT PHOTOS

1. What animal was on the cover of *The Most Beautiful Moment in Life Pt. 1* and *Pt. 2*? ....

2. Which album cover featured a colourful hot-air balloon? ....
....

3. The concept photos for which album saw BTS clad in double denim?
....

4. What colour was the cover art for 'Butter (Megan Thee Stallion Remix)'? ....

5. Which album artwork features a seaside bus shelter? ....
....

6. How many circles appear on the cover of *Wings*? ....

7. Concept photos for a version of which album featured the boys in bright red boxes surrounded by cameras, eyes, hands and amplifiers?
....

8. Which member oversaw the graphics and design of *BE*? ....

ANSWERS ON PAGE 216

9. The concept photos for which single featured the members washing cars outside a gas station? ....

10. The first concept photos for which album featured the group all dressed in white standing by a dark, ragged-edged hole in the wooden floor? ....

11. Which cover has a warning about the 'dangerous' effects of love?

....

12. Lyrics from which song appear on the *BE* album cover? ....

....

13. The concept photos for *BE* showed each member in a room styled by themselves. Whose room featured an array of footwear?

....

14. According to a scribble on an early mini-album cover what happens on 'Wed. 12. Feb.'? ....

15. How many times does the word 'Dynamite' appear on the cover artwork for the single? ....

FOOD

1. What did Jin eat in the July 2020 *Eat Jin* episode? ....

2. What kind of food was V's 'squirrel trapped in garden' in a 2017 *BTS Gayo* episode? ....

3. J-Hope lay in a room full of what kind of food in the 'Fake Love' MV?

   ....

4. Which member stood up and spelled out 'Pasta' and 'Pizza' in English in a V Live? ....

5. Jimin and V famously fell out (they soon made up) over whether they should eat what food before or after practice? ....

6. Which member is BTS's ramen expert? ....

7. *Burn The Stage* revealed that J-Hope and Jungkook once got in a fight over which fruit? ....

8. *Run BTS* episode 57 featured a cooking competition of what cuisine?

   ....

9. On *Bon Voyage* season 4, in New Zealand, which member cooks *kimchi jjigae* (kimchi stew) for the others? ....

10. What food gift did Halsey bring BTS after meeting them at the BBMAs in 2017? ....

11. BTS have expressed a love of which US fast-food chain that serves American-Chinese food? ....

12. In 'MIC Drop', what 'undercooked' food is mentioned by J-Hope, and what 'tasteless' or 'bad-tasting' food is mentioned by Suga?

....

13. Which member dressed as a vegetable in the 2016 Halloween dance-practice video of '21st Century Girl'? ....

14. In BTS's early days, what kind of restaurant did Suga and Jungkook discuss opening? ....

15. RM was mocked for the way he cut what at BTS's 1st birthday party?

....

ICONIC FASHION MOMENTS

BTS have had their fair share of iconic fashion moments
– can you guess who is who in the illustrations below?

1. ....

2. ....

3. ....

4. ....

5. ....

6. ....

7. ....

J-HOPE SOLO

1. What did international ARMY nickname J-Hope's solo release in the years preceding *Hope World*? ....

2. J-Hope released a full-length version of which song on the 3rd anniversary of *Hope World*? ....

3. Which boy-group rival did J-Hope take on in a dance battle at the 2015 K-Pop Dream Concert? ....

4. Which novel was one of the inspirations for *Hope World*? ....

....

5. J-Hope took on which global 2012 hit on BTS's karaoke night in a September 2021 episode of *Run BTS*? ....

6. Which J-Hope solo track features long-time BTS producer Supreme Boi? ....

7. Which J-Hope solo served as a comeback trailer for *Map of the Soul: 7*? ....

8. What does 'P.O.P' stand for in the title of *Hope World*'s second track? ....

9. What does 'Arthur' say to J-Hope during 'Daydream'? ....

10. Which BTS member makes a secret cameo in the 'Daydream' video?

....

11. What does J-Hope consume in his 'Airplane'? ....

12. J-Hope's first solo release sampled The Game & Skrillex's hit 'El Chapo'. What was it called? ....

13. What was the subject of J-Hope's full solo on *Wings*? ....

14. To which song did J-Hope dance solo on the *Wings* comeback trailer video? ....

15. Which song on the Love Yourself World Tour featured J-Hope's solo dance? ....

BANGTAN BOMBS, PART 2

1. In the 'Baepsae' dance-practice Bomb for the 2016 Festa, who loses the rock, paper, scissors game and has to perform the dance break?

    ....

2. Who is the magician in the 'BTS Magic Show' Bomb? ....

3. In the 'Let's Test BTS's Nerve!' Bomb, which two members – as predicted by the others – freak out at the disturbing image?

    ....

4. In the 2014 'Medley Show Time!' Bomb, V, Jimin, J-Hope, Jin and Suga dance and lip-sync to 'Sunset Glow' and 'Fantastic Baby' by which group? ....

5. When watching their DNA MV for the 'REAL reaction' Bomb in 2018, whose name does Suga famously shout? ....

6. In the ' "Dynamite" MV Reaction' Bomb, where does Suga say he thought the costumes were from? ....

7. Which 'Appeal version' Bomb saw them all performing in full *hanbok* (traditional Korean clothing)? ....

8. In the 2020 FESTA 'Map of the Song: 7' Bomb, which BTS solo track do RM and Jin sing at the karaoke? ....

9. Which pair cause sensible Jin to 'aekk' and 'eekk' during the 2021 Bomb 'Interview Squabble'? ....

10. Where were BTS in the 2021 'Dynamite' Bomb, which saw both J-Hope and V fall on the floor? ....

11. In the '2021 FESTA Exam Behind the Scenes' Bomb, V claims the exam is all a Big Hit plot to keep who apart? ....

12. A 2020 'BTS eating' Bomb asked how much *what* did Jungkook eat?

....

13. Which song do V and Jin sing in the 2018 'BTS Prom Party: Unit Stage' Bomb? ....

14. In the 2015 Bangtan Bomb featuring 'War of Hormone' (Real WAR version), who bangs his head on the ceiling and who looks like the chaos feels a little too much? ....

15. In which city did they film the Bomb called 'Show Me Your BBA SAE!?!?'? ....

LINES AND SUBUNITS

1. *Maknae* Line: ....

2. Daegu Line: ....

3. *Hyung* Line: ....

4. Busan Line: ....

5. Kim Line: ....

6. Rap Line: ....

7. 95 Line: ....

8. Vocal Line: ....

9. 94 Line: ....

10. Dance Line, aka 3J: ....

11. Visual Line, aka Bermuda Triangle: ....

12. Sope: ....

13. Minimini: ....

14. 2seok: ....

15. Minimoni: ....

Line: A 'line' is a K-pop term for linking together members of a group who have something in common: the singers, the dancers, those born in the same year or same city.

Subunit: These are smaller groups made up from the members. While BTS has no official subunits, that hasn't stopped ARMY naming their own.

Bermuda Triangle: another name for the Visual Line, so named because you get lost in and can't escape their good looks.

YOU KNOW BTS MUSIC VIDEOS? PART 2

1. The dance scenes from the 'MIC Drop (Steve Aoki Remix)' MV have the boys kitted out in which brand with a skull-and-crossbone logo? ....

2. In 'Fake Love', at the end of the hall where V is standing, the title of which BTS song is written in the window? ....

3. What animal appears in silhouette in the opening scene of the 'IDOL' MV? ....

4. What is the name of the cinema in the 'Boy with Luv' MV?

   ....

5. The boys practise the choreography to which song in the 'Heartbeat' MV? ....

6. In the 'Make It Right' MV, what turns back into a girl at the conclusion of the animation? ....

7. The 'ON' MV referenced many movies but a nod to which movie led to Jungkook being called Thomas? ....

8. Which member opens his wings in the 'Black Swan' MV? ....

9. What breed of dog appears in the 'Stay Gold' MV? ....

10. What two foods does the diner in 'Dynamite' offer? ....
....

11. What kind of houseplant is RM caring for in the 'Life Goes On' MV?
....

12. Which member has the number 384627 on his ID board in the 'Butter' MV? ....

13. According to the poster in the 'Permission to Dance' MV, who should we vote for as President of the Student Body? ....

14. What is the DJ's name in the 'My Universe' MV? ....

15. What does Jin hold up as the other members sit and talk in the 'Film Out' MV? ....

KOREAN WORDS AND PHRASES

1. What are BTS asking for us and them to be when they say 'haengbok haja'? ....

2. When BTS say 'annyeonghaseyo', what are they saying?

   ....

3. What Korean exclamation of encouragement do BTS use to say, 'Come on!' or 'Let's do it!'? ....

4. 'Satoori Rap' is a BTS rap battle between members from different parts of Korea. What does satoori mean? ....

5. Who should be addressed as hyung by a boy or man?.....................

   ....

6. What is the Korean word for a selfie?...

7. What is a chingu?..

8. As the youngest of the group, Jungkook is given what title?

....

9. *Baepsae* has a slang meaning of 'try-hard', but is also the Korean name of which bird? ....

10. What word does K-pop use to mean acting in a cute and innocent manner? ....

11. What name is given to the Grand Prize at a Korean awards ceremony (BTS have collected a record number of these)? ....

12. If Suga shouts 'so-ri jil-luh!' during a concert, what is he asking the audience to do? ....

13. What does *saranghae* mean? ....

14. The track '*Jageun geotdeureul wihan shi*' is called 'Boy with Luv' in English, but what is the literal translation? ....

....

15. What is the English translation of the surprised or pleased exclamation '*daebak!*'? ....

J-HOPE BIAS

1. How many piercings does J-Hope have?

2. With which BTS member did J-Hope perform 'Otsukare'?

3. 'When it comes to a show, there's none like . . .' – which legendary artist did J-Hope excitedly post photos on Instagram of him meeting backstage after their show?

4. J-Hope revealed he once nearly left BTS but the members persuaded him to stay. Was this pre-debut, in the *Wings* era or during the COVID-19 hiatus?

5. J-Hope was the subject of the most-liked tweet of 2018 in a clip showing him dance alongside a car. Which Twitter challenge was he taking part in?

6. J-Hope contributed to the writing of his own and which other solo track on *Wings*?

7. Which cover, posted on YouTube in 2015, did J-Hope perform with V?

8. Under what title does J-Hope occasionally post his dance-practice videos to social media? ....

9. Which designer brand was responsible for J-Hope's Love Yourself: Speak Yourself Tour 'Outro: Tear'/'MIC Drop' outfit, complete with chest harness and chains? ....

10. At which market did J-Hope 'meet' Suga on their V Live streams?

    ....

11. On which *BTS World* track did J-hope, V and Zara Larsson join forces? ....

12. Which US-based Latina singer collaborated with J-Hope on 'Chicken Noodle Soup'? ....

13. What colour was J-Hope's velvet suit when BTS performed 'Dynamite' at the 2020 MMAs? ....

14. With which member did J-Hope perform 'Feliz Navidad' for the BTS Christmas Medley at the 2019 SBS K-POP Awards? ....

15. Which fan-favourite track from *Map of the Soul: Persona* did RM say was largely written by J-Hope? ....

CRYPTIC CELEBRITY FANS

1. Fortunately, this singer has seven rings ready. ....

2. You don't want to get into a fight with this fella – he's been a big fan for years. ....

3. You can only 'wonder' if this singer might record a 'monster' hit with BTS one day. ....

4. She was busy thinking 'bout (Bangtan) boys when she captioned a photo of her and BTS with 'first day as the newest member of @BTS_twt. love u guys' in 2017. ....

5. They're not just 'rumors' – this singer performed a cover of 'Butter' in a bandeau top emblazoned with 'VMIN'. ....

6. This US talent-show host has shown she's a model fan.

    ....

7. He's a 'sucker' for the Bangtan Boys and so are his brothers Kevin and Nick. ....

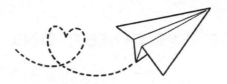

8. My oh my, if she didn't get the next seat to BTS at the 2019 Grammys . . . .

9. She admits that BTS were 'the favourite' when she hosted them on *Saturday Night Live.* ....

10. Alright, alright, alright, this 'gentleman' was spotted at the Love Yourself concert in Texas. ....

11. Whoopee! This actress gave the boys her shirt on *The Graham Norton Show.* ....

12. This UK rapper went down a storm when he attended a BTS concert in London. ....

13. Bet this maze runner was not the only teen wolf in the audience at a BTS concert in LA. ....

14. This *Game of Thrones* assassin has her eyes on Jungkook – but it's love, not revenge, she's after. ....

15. He might be a nonagenarian, but his long trek has led him to discover that BTS are out of this world. ....

BTS EXHIBITIONS

1. The Butterfly Dream Exhibition featured the making of which BTS EP/mini-album? ....

2. At the Butterfly Dream Exhibition, each member was linked to a coffee flavour – who was Caramel Latte, who was Americano and who chose Hazelnut Latte? ....

3. James Jean's *Seven Phases* artwork exhibited at the HYBE Insight Museum in 2021 featured members as spirits or mythic creatures. Which member was represented by a painting called *Champignon* (which means 'mushroom')? ....

4. Which animal featured in the artwork inspired by Jungkook in James Jean's *Seven Phases*? ....

5. A room at the HYBE Insight Museum had only flowers and greenery and a scent inspired by which song? ....

6. The 24/7=Serendipity Exhibition featured a painting by Jungkook of which member in their 'Wings Short Film' video? ....

7. Oh, Neul was a 2018 exhibition in Seoul featuring photos and videos taken of and by BTS members. By what anniversary-related title was it known in English? ....

8. How many cities around the world hosted CONNECT, BTS exhibitions? ....

9. Which city in mainland Europe was one of the CONNECT, BTS host cities? ....

10. *Fly with Aerocene Pacha* was a CONNECT, BTS project by Tomás Saraceno. What kind of flight was involved? ....

11. Which artist created *New York Clearing*, a maze of aluminium tubing, for CONNECT, BTS? ....

12. CONNECT, BTS in Seoul featured *Beyond the Scene*, Korean artist Yiyun Kang's warped and blended projected images of what?

....

13. The UNESCO exhibition 'Korea: Cubically Imagined' in Paris featured an open cube with three LED screens showing life-size BTS members performing which concert? ....

14. The 2021 Humble Souls Exhibition was a collaboration between BTS and which renowned graffiti artist? ....

15. Which BTS member was selected to provide the audio guide for the Humble Souls Exhibition? ....

BANGTAN BOYS IN LOVE

BTS have recorded more than ten songs with 'love' or 'luv' in the title. Can you name them all? (Of course you can!)

....

....

....

....

....

....

....

RUN BTS!

1. In episode 144 of *Run BTS*, the group were asked which performance they each thought ARMY consider the best. Which did they choose? ....

2. Episode 24 saw the boys set off on a 'night safari'. What did they encounter? ....

3. In episode 33 they hilariously had to pull expressions for the camera while doing what? ....

4. What was the name of the pretty new female student who became the focus of the boys' attention in a skit for episode 11? ....

5. Episode 109 found them providing voice-overs for movies – including *Zootopia*, where which members voiced Nick Wilde, Judy Hopps and Flash? ....

6. During the 'Entertainment Quiz Show' in episode 137, who did V and Jungkook phone for help? ....

7. In an unforgettable episode 31, the boys have to remember the words to the 'Tomato Song' after doing what? ....

8. On the water slide in episode 81, V keeps his promise by shouting what as he flies through the air? ....

9. Their game to see who would share rooms in Canada in episode 70 left which four members trying to sleep on one bed? ....
....

10. Episode 65, a classic, finds them being sprayed with water each time they use a keyword unknown to them. Whose keyword is 'Ha ha ha'? ....

11. Episode 63 is set in the classroom. Which member is the teacher and who, despite not wanting the job, is elected class president?
....

12. Who said '*lachimolala*' in episode 41's whisper challenge, and what should they have said? ....

13. In the sports competition for the 100th episode, what did the team names have in common? ....

14. In episode 97's pyjama party, what word was written on the underside of Jimin's left sock? ....

15. In the 'Summer Outing' episodes 83–85, which member do all the other members team up against to complete the huge inflatable obstacle course floating on a lake – and somehow still lose to?

....

NAME THE EVENT . . .

BTS have a huge list of achievements to their name, but can you name these two historic moments, pictured below?

1. ....

2. ....

ANSWERS ON PAGE 222

SPOT THE DIFFERENCE

BTS are always red-carpet ready – but how good are you at picking up on the details? Can you spot the seven changes we made to the second version of this photo of them at the BBMAs in 2018?

WHOSE IS WHOSE?

ARMY know BTS inside out and back to front –
can you name the member by the zoomed-in body part?

1. ....

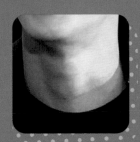

2. ....

3. ....

4. ....

6. ....

5. ....

7. ....

ANSWERS ON PAGE **222**

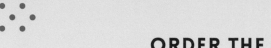

ORDER THE ERA . . .

The boys have been through a lot of eras – can you put these photos in chronological order, and for bonus points, name each era?

1. .... 2. ....

3. .... 4. ....

ANSWERS ON PAGE 223

C.

D.

GUESS-THE-HAIR

BTS have never been shy about the hair dye – can you name each member just from their rainbow-hued hair?

2. ....

3. ....

1. ....

4. ....

5. ....

7. ....

6. ....

ANSWERS ON PAGE 223

NAME THE EVENT . . .

Two more historic events to name below –
can you identify them?

1. ....

2. ....

ANSWERS ON PAGE 223

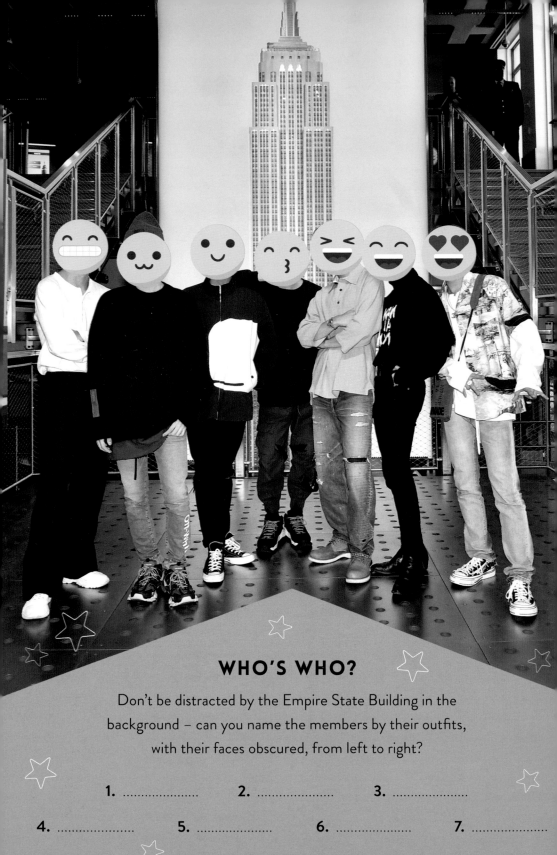

WHO'S WHO?

Don't be distracted by the Empire State Building in the background – can you name the members by their outfits, with their faces obscured, from left to right?

1. ....   2. ....   3. ....

4. ....   5. ....   6. ....   7. ....

ANSWERS ON PAGE **223**

IN A WORD

Many of BTS's English song titles are just a single word. How many can you list? (There are at least 50 to think of – and some of them are one word on one album but two words on other albums . . .)

RM IN FOCUS

1. What is RM's real name? ....

2. In what year was he born? ....

3. Which TV series does he credit with helping him learn English?

   ....

4. In which country did RM live for a few months when he was 12 years old? ....

5. What did RM design for the ARTIST-MADE merch collection released in 2022? ....

6. In BTS's early years, RM's clumsiness led him to be nicknamed 'God of . . .' what? ....

7. RM helped write 'Party (XXO)', the debut single for which girl group? ....

8. Which two BTS members have spent time as RM's roommate (after all seven of them shared one room)? ....

9. When BTS took a break in December 2021, RM travelled to see a small art museum in which US state? ....

10. Which member of GOT7 is said to be a friend of RM?

    ....

11. In 2018 RM had medical surgery on which part of his body – his ears, his eyes or his nose? ....

12. Which two European countries did RM visit on a family holiday in 2017? ....

13. What did RM lose in Sweden and in Chile? ....

14. What sport did RM claim was the only one he was ever any good at?

    ....

15. Complete RM's iconic quote: 'Y'all know my name is Rap Monster, not . . .' ....

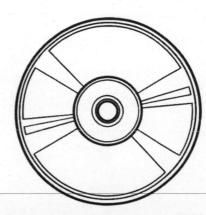

FUNNY OUTFITS

All the members love to look stylish, but they're not
afraid of looking silly or cute to make ARMY laugh,
either – can you match the outfits to the members?

1. ....

2. ....

3. ....

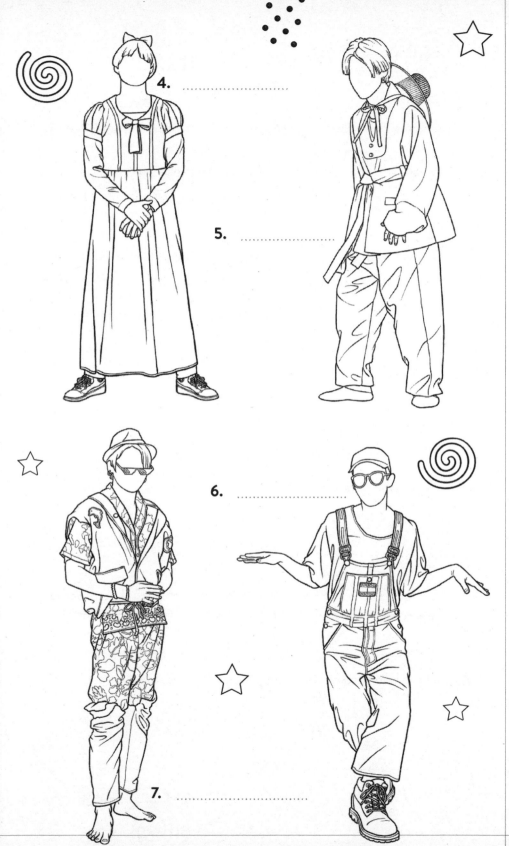

4. ....

5. ....

6. ....

7. ....

TRIVIA

1. Which two BTS members did RM reveal the singer Lizzo was particularly keen on after they met at a Harry Styles concert?

   ....

2. During lockdown in 2020 V suggested people share what they want to do after the pandemic ends – under what title did the proposal go viral? ....

3. Which member choreographed the end-of-show dance when 'Spring Day' won Music Bank? ....

4. Which BTS music video was directed by Jungkook? ....

5. On the Wings Tour, in which country did RM announce he wanted to live if he couldn't live in Korea? ....

6. Jungkook's walk at the 2018 MAMAs became a viral meme when set to which non-BTS hit? ....

7. Whose solo song did Suga sing at the 2017 Festa? ....

ANSWERS ON PAGE 218–19

8. The Bangtan Bomb of behind-the-scenes moments from their 'Dynamite' performance at *The Tonight Show Starring Jimmy Fallon* revealed which two members having trouble staying upright at the roller-skating rink? ....

9. At the Louis Vuitton Men's Fashion Show of Fall–Winter 2021, which member stole headlines with his gold wraparound orange-tinted shades? ....

10. When The Chainsmokers played in Seoul in 2017, BTS joined them on stage to perform which song? ....

11. In which city did Halsey first perform live with BTS? ....

12. Which megastar singer posted a TikTok of himself taking on the BTS #ButterChallenge? ....

13. Which minute-long song – with a nod to his love of fishing – did Jin drop to celebrate his birthday in 2021? ....

14. In 2018, after being invited by Stevie Wonder, BTS took part in the Dream Still Lives project honouring which iconic figure?

....

15. The book *I Decided to Live as Me* became a bestseller in South Korea and Japan after which member recommended it in 2019?

....

JIMIN SOLO

1. Which Jimin solo track appeared on the BTS album *Wings*?

    ....

2. To what track did a white-clad Jimin dance solo at the 2019 MMAs?

    ....

3. In Jimin's 'Filter', which kind of magical figure did he offer to be?

    ....

4. Who took the cover photo for Jimin's solo single 'Promise'?

    ....

5. Jimin posted an a cappella version of which song from *Dark & Wild*
    on the BTS fancafe? ....

6. Which celebration song did Jimin sing with V in February 2014?

    ....

7. Jimin wrote the words for which 2014 festive song?..................

8. Which member of BTS helped Jimin write the lyrics to 'Promise'?

    ....

9. On which album did Jimin's track 'Serendipity' first appear?

....

10. What colour were the two different suits that Jimin wore for his performance of 'Filter' during the livestreamed Map of the Soul ON:E concerts in 2020? ....

11. What is the name of the Jimin's theme on the *BTS World: Original Soundtrack*? ....

12. In what year did Jimin write and record 'Christmas Love' as a gift to ARMY? ....

13. By August 2021, how many combined streams had Jimin's solo songs amassed on SoundCloud, Spotify and YouTube: 100 million, 500 million or 1 billion? ....

14. Which Jimin video features a cat called Curry?.............................

15. What fruit does Jimin eat at the end of the video for 'Lie'?..................

JAPAN, PART 2

1. Jin surprised everyone by reading out a letter to whom at the Japan Showcase in 2014? ....

2. How many tracks are there on the physical edition of BTS's Japanese compilation album *BTS, the Best*? ....

3. The absence of which two members through illness caused BTS to cancel concerts in Kobe in 2015? ....

4. Which two songs did they perform on the first of those Kobe dates before abandoning the show? ....

5. Which two members were involved in *GCF in Tokyo*? ....
....

6. In the 'For You' music video, which member works at a gas station and who waits on tables? ....

7. 'Chi, Ase, Namida' is the Japanese title of which song? ....
....

8. 'Good Day' and 'Wishing on a Star' appeared on which album?

....

9. 'Peppuse' is the Japanese version of which song? ....

10. What was the lead single from *Map of the Soul: 7 – The Journey*?

....

11. 'Your Eyes Tell' from *Map of the Soul: 7 – The Journey* was written by which member? ....

12. Which track on *Youth* mentions each of the group by name?

....

13. For which track was Jin praised for singing a triple high note live on a TV performance in Japan? ....

14. In Sapporo, Japan, RM injured which part of his body when he bumped into a piece of furniture? ....

15. Did the official Japanese video for 'Airplane Pt. 2' mainly take place in a bar, on an aeroplane or in a record store? ....

FESTIVE BTS

1. What Christmas song did BTS record before they even debuted?

   ....

2. What item of clothing did the group all wear for their 'Butter (Holiday Remix)' dance-practice video? ....

3. Jungkook and Jimin's 'Christmas Day' was based on which song?

   ....

4. Which member celebrates his birthday between Christmas and New Year? ....

5. Which solo self-penned song mentions 'Christmas', 'Santa Claus' and 'mistletoe'? ....

6. Which solo track recalls the first time seeing thick snow falling and states a desire for Christmas to last forever? ....

7. In which iconic landmark did BTS perform for *Dick Clark's New Year's Rockin' Eve with Ryan Seacrest* to bring in 2020?

   ....

8. Which two members joined up with then Big Hit Entertainment artists Jo Kwon, Lim Jeong-hee and Joo Hee for 'Perfect Christmas' in 2013? ....

9. Which track did Jin post a Christmas version of for 'Jinsta' (his birthday celebration) on SoundCloud in December 2016? ....

10. Which holiday favourite did a mask-wearing BTS sing on the red carpet at the 2020 *SBS Gayo Daejeon*? ....

11. Who uploaded a cover of a 19th-century carol (albeit following the style of indie acoustic-pop duo J Rabbit) on Christmas Eve in 2017?

....

12. At the 2019 *SBS Gayo Daejeon*, which members sang 'Jingle Bell Rock'? ....

13. A 2015 Bangtan Bomb featured the boys in Christmas earmuffs, hats and headbands lip-syncing to which of their songs?

....

14. With which song did BTS get the Christmas spirit flowing in *Disney's Holiday Singalong* in 2020? ....

15. In 'Dynamite (Holiday Remix)', which word did RM substitute for the original 'medicine'? ....

LOVE YOURSELF ERA

1. Which BTS song was played at the opening ceremony of the 2018 Winter Olympics? ....

2. Which song mentions a style of music common to Mexico?

....

3. Which costumes did the group wear while performing 'Anpanman' at the 2018 Festa? ....

4. What was the name of the remix of 'Spring Day' that was played at the 2017 KBS Song Festival and released in June 2018?

....

5. What sequel to 'Save Me' appeared on *Love Yourself: Answer*?

....

6. Which song on *Love Yourself: Her* was a collaboration with US duo The Chainsmokers? ....

7. In the *Break The Silence* docu-series, what did the group reveal as the inspiration behind 'Outro: Tear'? ....

8. '134340', a track on *Love Yourself: Tear*, is associated with which celestial body? ....

9. What is 'smeraldo' and which member is associated with it in this era?

....

10. What dance craze did the group (especially Jungkook) incorporate into the 'Go Go' choreography? ....

11. Which song was banned for broadcast in South Korea as it mentioned Twitter and V App (aka V Live)? ....

12. Which song closed the *Love Yourself* series and was the final song on the Love Yourself World Tour setlist? ....

13. Where did BTS first perform 'Fake Love'? ....

14. Which rap-line track did BTS release on their SoundCloud as part of their 5th-anniversary 'Festa' celebration? ....

15. Which title was inspired by an action of former US president Barack Obama? ....

BRAND PARTNERSHIPS AND ACCIDENTAL ENDORSEMENTS

1. Which shoe company were named in the title of a BTS song?

   ....

2. The chant of '*eogiyeongcha*' was a large part of the soundtrack to a BTS video with which campaign? ....

3. Which song did BTS record to help promote the Hyundai IONIQ?

   ....

4. Which female rapper collaborated with BTS in a 2016 TV commercial for 'SK Telecom'? ....

5. Which sports clothing company launched a 'BTS Dynamite Collection' in 2021? ....

6. In 2021, Lotte Duty Free's social media channels broadcast a three-episode sitcom featuring BTS. What was the title? ....

7. What accessory worn by Jimin in BTS's 2019 BBMAs performance of 'Boy with Luv' rapidly sold out? ....

8. Which SUV did BTS step out from during the 2019 Grammy Awards?

....

9. Who inadvertently launched a rush on fabric softener in answering a question on BTS's fancafe? ....

10. In BTS's deal with Baskin-Robbins, each member chose their favourite flavour. Who chose Almond Bong Bong and who picked New York Cheesecake? ....

11. In 2020, BTS teamed up with the company Bodyfriend to promote what product? ....

12. What V-designed product reportedly sold out in less than a minute in January 2022? ....

13. Which fast-food chain's 'BTS meal' included cajun and sweet chilli sauce? ....

14. Which fashion house signed BTS as global ambassadors in 2021?

....

15. Which piece of Map of the Soul ON:E merch did J-Hope manage to sell out in minutes with a single tweet? ....

VARIETY AND REALITY SHOWS

1. Shortly after their debut, BTS starred in their own variety series, playing games and taking on challenges. What was the series called?

   ....

2. Which BTS member was among the 'men with hot brains' on the talk show *Problematic Men*? ....

3. Which member performed the choreography to 'Boy in Luv' at half and double speeds on *Weekly Idol*? ....

4. Where was *American Hustle Life* filmed? ....

5. On which show set in a schoolroom did V re-enact a scene from the movie *Wish*? ....

6. On the show *Please Take Care of My Refrigerator*, Jin confessed that BTS's fridge was mainly full of what? ....

7. In which 2021 variety show did BTS meet Kim Jung-hyun, the girl who had gone viral with her dance to 'MIC Drop' in 2017?

   ....

8. What song did Jungkook (aka 'Fencing Man') sing on *The Masked Singer*? ....

9. V's friendship with actor Kim Min-jae was the focus of season 1 of which show? ....

10. In the 300th episode of which show did BTS appear and compete against the cast in a mission of moving ramyeon boxes across a sports field? ....

11. Which 2021 K-pop talent-show finale featured BTS giving advice to the newly formed boy group Enhypen? ....

12. Which BTS member took part in the survival game show *Law of the Jungle*? ....

13. J-Hope appeared as a dance teacher in which 2019 TV show?

....

14. Which three members took part in an episode of *My Pet Clinic*?

....

15. In which reality show based around BTS's trip to KCon in 2014 did Jungkook refer to himself as 'International Playboy'? ....

SIGNATURE POSES

Can you tell which BTS member is which
from their signature poses below?

1. ....

2. ....

3. ....

4. ....

5. ....

6. ....

7. ....

WEBTOONS AND BT21

1. The webtoon *Hip Hop Monsters* featured RM as a duck, Jin as a wolf, Suga as a turtle, J-Hope as a horse . . . What were Jimin, V and Jungkook? ....

2. What was the full name of the *We On* webtoon? ....

3. In *We On*, who or what are attacking the world? ....

4. In the *Save Me* webtoon, who saves Yoon-gi from the burning building? ....

5. In *Save Me*, what kind of disorder does Ho-seok suffer from? ....

6. Can you name the eight main BT21 characters? ....

7. Whose BT21 character is a sleepy blue koala? ....

8. Which character represents ARMY and protects BT21?

....

9. Which BT21 character has a blue outfit with yellow dots?

....

10. Which track did BTS perform at their 2018 Prom Party and in a Halloween dance practice dressed as their BT21 characters?

....

11. Which two BT21 characters' costumes has Suga had to wear as *Run BTS* punishments? ....

12. In which fictional city is *7 Fates: Chakho* set? ....

13. Which old Korean word for 'tiger' is the name given to the supernatural tigers from Korean folklore that appear in *7 Fates: Chakho*? ....

14. Which character falls in love with one of these creatures in *7 Fates: Chakho*? ....

15. Which member plays the half-human, half-tiger character Zeha in *7 Fates: Chakho*? ....

JIN SOLO

1. Jin released a solo song on SoundCloud for the 2019 Festa – what was its title? ....

2. The Jin solo 'Epiphany' appeared on which album?.........................

3. What did Jin say was his inspiration for writing 'Abyss'?.....................
....

4. In 2018, Jin covered which 1994 song by Korean rock legend Yoon Do-hyun? ....

5. What cover song did Jin release as a gift for Parents' Day in 2015?
....

6. What instrument does Jin play when he performs 'Epiphany' live?
....

7. In which year did Jin upload 'I Love You' for ARMY on his birthday?
....

8. What was the first solo song that Jin co-produced and co-wrote?

....

9. Which Christmas saw the release of a festive version of 'Awake'?

....

10. Which Jin solo song became the most commented audio in YouTube history? ....

11. Which song, that he created the unofficial choreography for, did Jin dance solo to at BTS's 5th Muster in 2019? ....

12. To which song did Jin dance solo to at the 2019 MMAs?

....

13. To whom did Jin dedicate his solo song 'Moon'?..................................

14. What was the theme of the room Jin designed for his *BE* concept photos? ....

15. What did Jin say he feared his company would want if the #SuperTunaChallenge was too successful? ....

COLLABORATIONS

1. In 2016, BTS joined forces with which group to record 'Family Day' for the Family Love Day campaign? ....

2. Lauv's song 'Who' featured which members of BTS? ....
   ....

3. Which country singer joined BTS and Lil Nas X on stage at the 2020 Grammy Awards? ....

4. Which BTS hit was co-written by a member of rock group Snow Patrol? ....

5. Which rapper added a guest verse to a remix of 'Butter'? ....
   ....

6. Which collaboration track appears on the album *Music of the Spheres*? ....

7. BTS collaborated with Steve Aoki for 'MIC Drop', 'Waste It on Me' and which other track? ....

8. Which song's remix featured Nicki Minaj? ....

9. Rapper Juice WRLD teamed up with RM and Suga on which track from *BTS World: Original Soundtrack?* ....

10. According to Chris Martin, whose idea was it that Coldplay collaborate with BTS? ....

11. BTS worked with Sia on which song? ....

12. Which three members of BTS featured on a remix of Jawsh 685 and Jason Derulo's 'Savage Love (Laxed – Siren Beat)'? ....

   ....

13. What did Halsey gift all the BTS members before their joint performance at the 2019 BBMAs? ....

14. BTS shared a collaborative stage the 2015 MAMAs with which hip-hop idol group? ....

15. Who was credited as a writer on 'Make It Right': Ed Sheeran, Chris Martin or Eminem? ....

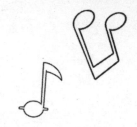

INSTRUMENTS

1. On what instrument did V perform 'Twinkle Twinkle Little Star' for the rest of the group on his birthday on 30 December 2019?

    ....

2. A 2021 promotional video for the city called 'Your Seoul Goes On' featured Jungkook playing which instrument? ....

3. Which member of BTS claimed to have 'forgotten' how to play guitar in an attempt to get Coldplay's Chris Martin to teach him?

    ....

4. Which member is BTS's beatbox king? ....

5. What colour was the ukulele Jin played in a later-deleted V Live?

    ....

6. BTS released an orchestral version of which song in 2020?

    ....

7. What instrument did V demonstrate his expertise in on the TV show *Star Show 360?* ....

8. The sound of which wind instrument features heavily on '134340'?

   ....

9. A 'Hwagae Market' Sope V Live saw J-Hope playing 'My Heart Will Go On' on what instrument and in what unusual style? ....

   ....

10. Which two members pick up the guitar to play in the Bangtan Bomb 'Live Guitar Show at the Roller Rink'? ....

11. Which BTS song features the *kkwaenggwari* and other traditional Korean instruments? ....

12. The Bangtan Bomb 'Let's Play Guitar' features Jimin playing guitar and Jungkook singing along to which Justin Bieber song?

    ....

13. In the same Bangtan Bomb, V attempts to play Jason Mraz's 'I'm Yours' on what instrument? ....

14. Who played guitar on the acoustic version of 'Boy in Luv' at the Japanese Fan Meeting in 2017? ....

15. V had lessons in which instrument during the second season of *In the Soop*? ....

NO. 1s

1. BTS were the first-ever act to have how many songs reach No. 1 on the iTunes charts in 100 countries around the world? ....

2. What was BTS's first No. 1 album in the US? ....

3. Which country was the first to see a BTS single at No. 1 in the official charts? ....

4. Which single was the first to hit No. 1 in South Korea? ....
....

5. Which V solo beat 'Black Swan' to top the iTunes chart in most (114) countries? ....

6. Did BTS first top the Billboard World Digital Song Sales chart with 'I Need U', 'Dope' or 'Fire'? ....

7. What was BTS's first No. 1 hit in Japan? ....

8. Which track was the first Korean OST (theme song) to enter Spotify's Top 50 Global chart and went to No. 1 in over 80 countries? ....

9. What was their first No. 1 in South Korea with a featured artist?

....

10. What was their first album to top the UK album chart? ....

....

11. For how many months did Jimin top the K-pop idol Brand Reputation Rankings list from December 2018 and to whom did he (briefly) relinquish the crown? ....

12. Was *BE* the group's third, fourth or fifth No. 1 album on the Billboard 200? ....

13. Which album was BTS's first chart topper in Ireland, Belgium, France, Germany and the Netherlands? ....

14. Which BTS solo track reached iTunes No. 1 in 100 countries in the shortest period of time? ....

15. Which viral song's BTS-featuring remix went to No. 1 on the Billboard chart in 2020? ....

TRUE OR FALSE?

1. Jin once named the BTS groupchat 'Seokjin and the 6 babies'.

2. Jimin's tweet saying just the word 'I' was retweeted over a million times.

3. V took up golf in January 2022.

4. BTS originally had nine members but dropped two in order to be different from EXO.

5. At one time BTS were going to be called 'Big Kids'.

6. As a game punishment, Suga once had to dress in a frilly maid outfit and serve customers in a café.

7. Jimin once kept two pet axolotls.

8. BTS once performed a concert in front of the Kremlin in Moscow.

9. Jungkook once saved the life of a television host who fell into the hole created by a stage lift. ....

10. RM has written a book titled *The Gifts of Imperfection*. ....

11. Suga once said he thought 'Bambi' was the English word for 'deer'.

....

12. BTS played at the Pyeongchang Winter Olympics closing ceremony.

....

13. J-Hope likes to make friendship bracelets for the members and for ARMY. ....

14. Suga once fought with EXO's Baekhyun at the MAMAs. ....

15. BTS agreed to split shortly after their debut but were persuaded to stay together by J-Hope. ....

'DYNAMITE', *BE* AND 'BUTTER'

1. What new hair colours did RM and V reveal in the first teasers for 'Dynamite'? ....

2. Who gives V a playful cuff for staying in pose too long at the end of the 'Dynamite' B-side MV? ....

3. To which international headquarters did BTS return in September 2020 to speak about the COVID-19 pandemic? ....

4. Which members of the group perform the track 'Stay' on *BE*?

....

5. Which two songs did BTS perform at Gyeongbokgung Palace in Seoul for *The Tonight Show Starring Jimmy Fallon* in November 2020?

....

6. In November 2020, BTS received their first Grammy nomination for their music. In which category were they nominated? ....

....

7. BTS headlined Big Hit's 2021 New Year's Eve concert, performing a collaboration trilogy as a finale. This included an acoustic version of which song? ....

8. BTS self-produced their album *BE* with members having different responsibilities. Who was in charge of A&R, liaising with Big Hit management? ....

9. For which broadcast did BTS first perform 'Life Goes On'?

....

10. Which track on *BE* credits Australian duo Cosmo's Midnight as producers and co-writers? ....

11. What feat do BTS celebrate on the *BE* track 'Skit'?.................

12. What happened in the hour-long 'Butter' teaser that dropped on YouTube in April 2021? ....

13. Which member forms the 'R' when BTS spell out 'ARMY' in their 'Butter' choreography? ....

14. In the concept photos for 'Butter', which member posed in massive fur boots and a kilt-style skirt? ....

15. In which city did BTS perform Permission to Dance on Stage, their first concert in front of a live audience since before the pandemic began?

....

SET LIST

In October 2020, BTS performed Map of the Soul ON:E at the Olympic Gymnastics Arena, Seoul, with both nights streamed online. The selection of songs performed was the same on both dates except for the encores. Can you fill in the blanks to complete the setlist?

1. _N

2. N._

3. _ _ _r_ B_ _ _ _ _ _ _ _ _ f P_. _

4. Intro: P_ _ _ _ _ _

5. _ _ _ _ _ Lu_

6. D_ _ _ _ _ _ _

7. Int_ _ _ _ _ _: S_ _d_w

8. B_ _ _ _ S_ _ _

9. _ _ _!

10. _ _:_ _ (Z_ _ _ _'C_ _ _ _)

11. M_ _ _me

12. _ _ _ter

13. M_ _ _

14. I_ _ _r _ _ _ _d

15. O_ _ _ _: _ _o

16. _ _ _ _ _ _ _ Lu_

17. D_ _

18. D_ _ _

19. No _ _ _ _ _ _ _am

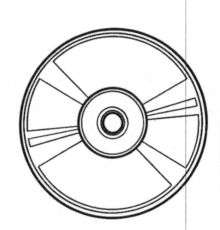

ENCORE NIGHT ONE

20. B_ _ _ _rf_ _

21. R_ _

22. _y_ _ _i_ _

23. _ _ _ _ _ _ul_ _ _p_ _ _ _: _h_ _ _er_ _ _

ENCORE NIGHT TWO

24. _ _ _ _ _g _a_

25. I_ _ _

26. D_ _ _i_ _

27. _e _r_ B_ _ _e_ _ _oo_: t_ _ _t_ _n_ _

JUNGKOOK IN FOCUS

1. What is Jungkook's full name? ....

2. In what year was he born? ....

3. In which city did he grow up? ....

4. How many sisters and/or brothers does he have? ....

5. What domestic duty did Jungkook seem obsessed with on *American Hustle Life*? ....

6. At what age did Jungkook get his driving licence? ....

7. What nickname did RM give to Jungkook because of his ripped body?

   ....

8. Which relative of Jungkook appeared in '[EPISODE] Jung Kook went to High school with BTS!' on YouTube? ....

9. In a Q&A game for *Tokopedia*, which song did Jungkook say best represented his true self? ....

10. In June 2019 Jungkook posted a tweet captioned 'Duh!' which gained over 1.7 million likes in 24 hours. What song was he lip-syncing and dancing to? ....

11. Jungkook and GOT7's Yugyeom have two matching tattoos – one is an ox (as they were both born in the Year of the Ox), but what is the other one? ....

12. What colour co-ord did Jungkook wear during his V Live 'mini-concert' in August 2021 (which also made an appearance on season 2 of *In the Soop*)? ....

13. Talos's 'To Each His Own' is used as the soundtrack for which GCF production? ....

14. Which of Jungkook's piercings was fake for the 'Butter' MV but later done for real? ....

15. What Nirvana song lyrics and life motto does Jungkook have tattooed on his arm? ....

SOCIAL MEDIA

1. Under which hashtag did BTS's outcry against racist abuse become the most retweeted tweet of 2021? ....

2. What colour were V's glasses in the 'accidental selfie' posted on Twitter in 2017? ....

3. BTS fans mashed up which dance trend with BTS's 'Black Swan' in a viral TikTok? ....

4. Which J-Hope solo track produced a TikTok dance challenge in 2019? ....

5. What did Jungkook tweet in January 2021 that got over 3 million likes? ....

6. What did V tweet under a photo of him looking at a Simpsons-style portrait of him? ....

7. Which member's bending of the truth was exposed by his bandmates when he posted a 'candid' photo of himself? ....

8. RM tweeted a new nickname for Suga, 'Min Deolleong' ('Min Clumsy'), that went viral after Suga did what in January 2018?

....

9. In February 2022, Jungkook captioned an Instagram video with the phrase 'My body feels heavy now . . .' – which song was he dancing *Street Dance Girls Fighter*'s Nain's choreography to? ....

....

10. In what year did BTS first become the most mentioned celebrities on Twitter globally? ....

11. Which member's concept photo for 'Butter' was the official BTS Instagram account's most liked post? ....

12. Which BTS-related hashtag set a world record as most mentioned on both TikTok and Twitter? ....

13. On 6 December 2021, the BTS members finally opened individual accounts on Instagram. What handles did they each originally pick?

....

....

14. After accidentally deleting his first Instagram post, Suga's next was a red square with a caption saying IG was what? ....

15. RM's first Instagram post was of him sitting by the sea in which location? ....

BIG HIT

1. Big Hit founder Bang Si-hyuk is also known by which nicknames?

   ....

2. In what year was Big Hit formed? ....

3. Bang made his name as a producer of which first-generation K-pop group's debut album *Chapter One*? ....

4. Big Hit's first group was 8Eight – what kind of group were they?

   ....

5. In 2012 Big Hit signed their first girl group. What was their name?

   ....

6. In 2007 producer Kang Hyo-won began working for Big Hit. He would be a major part of BTS's success, under what name? ....

   ....

7. Which boy group did Big Hit co-manage with JYP Entertainment from 2010 to 2014? ....

8. Which Big Hit duo disbanded eight years after their 2010 No. 1 hit 'I Was Able to Eat Well'? ....

9. Which fan community platform was launched by Big Hit in 2019?

....

10. Which girl group made their Korean comeback after the acquisition of Source Music by Big Hit in 2019? ....

11. What is the full name of TXT, the Big Hit boy group who debuted in March 2019? ....

12. Which BTS member contributed to the writing of TXT's 'OX1=Lovesong (I Know I Love You)'? ....

13. In 2021, Big Hit Entertainment became a sub-label as part of what newly formed corporation? ....

14. Which boy group, signed to one of the corporation's sub-labels, was formed through the 2020 survival competition show *I-Land*?

....

15. Seventeen and Nu'Est became associated with BTS when Big Hit became majority shareholders of which record label in 2020?

....

V LIVE AND WEVERSE

1. Where did *BTS Bokbukbok* – their V Live series in which they played fun games – take place? ....

2. Which pairing announced their split and reunion in the 'Hwagae Market Disbandment' prank video on V Live? ....

3. What was the name of V's radio station on V Live?...................

4. RM gave Jungkook some English-language tuition in what occasional V Live series? ....

5. Whose 2021 mini-concert on V Live included covers of Blackbear, Bruno Mars and Justin Bieber, as well as a number of BTS songs?

   ....

6. What did RM and J-Hope decorate in their 2020 V Live arts and crafts session that was crashed by Jungkook? ....

7. Which member receives so many marriage proposals – even on other members' V Lives – that it has become an in-joke, and led to him pointing out after the Grammys in 2022 that anyone can get married at a drive-thru in Las Vegas? ....

8. Which member told V and Jungkook to go to bed after he was woken by notifications from their late-night Weverse session? ....

9. After persuading Weverse to let BTS alter their profile details, to what did V change his photo and name? ....

10. What part-selfie pose of J-Hope's led to the other members posting pics imitating him? ....

11. On Weverse, RM replied to a fan who was sad over failing their driving test with the phrase: 'at least this planet has . . .' How did it end?

....

12. What did V tell Weverse he was doing that caused the platform to crash in January 2020? ....

13. What did RM say he wanted to eat that began a Weverse party?

....

14. 'I'll forward it – reply takes about two weeks.' What was V forwarding and to whom? ....

15. Jin used Weverse to try to stop people doing what challenge?

....

ANSWERS

DEBUT INTRODUCTIONS

1. Jungkook, 2. Jimin, 3. V,
4. J-Hope, 5. RM, 6. Jin, 7. Suga.

THE ONLY MEMBER WHO ...

1. V, 2. J-Hope, 3. Suga, 4. Jin,
5. RM, 6. J-Hope, 7. Suga, 8. RM,
9. Jimin, 10. Jungkook, 11. V,
12. Jimin, 13. Jungkook, 14. Jin, 15. V,
16. J-Hope.

ANIMALS

1. *Love Yourself: Tear*, 2. A rabbit,
3. J-Hope and Nuri, 4. A corgi,
5. Cats, 6. Shinhwa's Minwoo,
7. Brandley, 8. A crow, 9. A calico
cat, 10. A parrot, 11. 'Butter',
12. Snakes, 13. New Zealand,
14. BTS 4th Muster in 2018, 15. A
sugar glider and a shark.

JIN BIAS

1. Lilies, 2. Jin's brother, Kim Seok-
jung, on Instagram, 3. Snowboarding,
4. 'Car Door Guy', 5. Jin Hit
Entertainment, 6. Banana, 7. 'Why
does it get harder?', 8. BTS,
9. Mario, 10. In the show's group
photo, 11. As a Trojan Horse, 12. Suga
aka Agust D's 'Daechwita', 13. An
ARMY Bomb, 14. 'Stay', 15. Dad
(*ahjae*/uncle) jokes.

SCHOOL TRILOGY ERA

1. June 2013, 2. 'I Like it', 3. 'N.O',
4. J-Hope, 5. His trousers fell down,
6. V, 7. Jin, 8. 'Boy in Luv',
9. MAMA, 10. His underwear,
11. White, 12. 'Attack on Bangtan'
(aka 'Rise of Bangtan'), 13. 'Just One
Day', 14. Dracula (a vampire),
15. Vietnam.

PERSONALITY TYPES

1. RM and Jungkook, 2. Pig,
3. Hufflepuff, 4. Gryffindor,
5. Jin, 6. J-Hope, 7. Jin, 8. Jimin,
9. Jungkook, 10. Jungkook, 11. Jimin,
12. Capricorn, 13. RM, 14. Suga,
15. Jimin and Suga.

NICKNAMES

1. 'Nochu', 2. J-Hope, 3. 'Worldwide
Handsome', 4. RM (Namjoon),
5. 'Hobi', 6. 'Lil Meow Meow', 7. V,
8. 'Justin Seagull' (Jungkook),
9. Mochi, 10. 'Soondoongie', 11. RM,
12. Jin, RM, Jimin, 13. Suga,
14. 'Gucci Boy', 15. Jimin.

SUGA IN FOCUS

1. Basketball, 2. 'Wine' by Suran,
3. Delivery driver, 4. Shoulder,
5. Min Yoon-gi, 6. Dance, 7. 1993,
8. 'Slug', 9. Samsung Galaxy,
10. 'Trivia: Seesaw', 11. Mental illness,
12. IU's 'Eight', 13. Epik High,
14. 'Outro: Tear', 15. Older brother.

BTS VOCALS

1. V, 2. Jin, 3. Jimin and Jin, 4. He whispers his name, 5. 'Fake Love', 6. Tenor, 7. Coldplay's 'Fix You', 8. V, 9. 'Dionysus', 10. 'Airplane Pt. 2', 11. 'Spring Day', 12. Jimin, 13. 'Dis-ease', 14. Scat, 15. Adora.

RM SOLO

1. Joon-dogg, 2. Warren G, 3. 'Fantastic', 4. 'Seoul Town Road', 5. A classroom, 6. Seoul and Tokyo, 7. 'Monster', 8. 'God Rap', 9. 'Forever Rain', 10. eAeon, 11. 'Bicycle', 12. 'Change', 13. 'Moonchild', 14. 'Winter Flower', 15. Fall Out Boy.

ALTERNATIVE JOBS

1. RM, 2. Jimin, 3. Suga, 4. V, 5. J-Hope, 6. Jin, 7. Jungkook.

BANGTAN BOMBS, PART 1

1. Jungkook and Jimin, 2. Jimin and V, 3. J-Hope and Suga sang Homme's 'I Was Able to Eat Well', 4. '... of BTS', 5. In a hotel corridor, 6. 'Let's Speak English', 7. 'N.O', 8. 'BTS' rhythmical farce! LOL', 9. Snow White and the Six Dwarfs with V as Snow White, 10. It was an 'eye contact' version, 11. 'Coming of Age Ceremony', 12. 'Just One Day', 13. V, Jimin, RM, Suga, J-Hope, Jin and Jungkook, 14. V and Suga, 15. Cowboy on a horse, a cabbage.

JUNGKOOK BIAS

1. 'Decalcomania', 2. Right, 3. Milk, 4. Bluetooth speakers, 5. Yugyeom, 6. ARMY (with an uncrossed 'A'), 7. Left cheek, 8. Modern *hanbok* (traditional Korean clothing), 9. 'live without passion', 10. Took them to a Chinese restaurant, 11. 'International Playboy', 12. Microwave ovens, 13. 'Pardon', 14. 'ON' (a song they hadn't, at that point, been able to perform in front of ARMY), 15. Just walked down the long stage.

ONLY ARMY KNOW ...

1. 'Strong power thank you', 2. Jungshook, 3. Suga – 'inspires', 4. Jungkook, 5. Rrrrrap Monster, 6. 'I hate snakeu', 7. 'International Pop-K Sensation Sunshine Rainbow Traditional Transfer USB Hub Shrimp BTS', 8. Hungry, 9. 'Excuse me', 10. Saliva, 11. 'Spring Day', 12. '... Oh my God!', 13. 'Stob it!', 14. ARMY, 15. Jungkook and Suga.

SHOW ME YOUR MOVES

1. 'Permission to Dance', 2. 'MIC Drop', 3. 'Anpanman', 4. 'IDOL', 5. 'Silver Spoon' ('Baepsae').

WHO SINGS THE FIRST LINE?

1. V, 2. Jimin, 3. Jin, 4. Suga, 5. Jungkook, 6. J-Hope, 7. Jin,

8. Suga, 9. RM, 10. RM, 11. RM, 12. Suga, 13. Jimin, 14. J-Hope, 15. V.

WHO SAID WHAT?

1. RM, 2. V, 3. Jin, 4. J-Hope, 5. Suga, 6. Jungkook, 7. RM, 8. RM, 9. V, 10. Jimin, 11. Jin, 12. Suga, 13. V, 14. Jungkook, 15. Jin.

INFLUENCES

1. J-Hope, 2. BoA, 3. J-Hope and V, 4. Suga, 5. V, 6. Jungkook, 7. Seo Taiji & Boys, 8. Drake, 9. Ariana Grande, 10. Rain, 11. Jin, 12. Jungkook and V, 13. Jungkook, 14. Usher, 15. Big Bang.

V BIAS

1. 'Lovely Jubbly', 2. 'Gucci', 3. Lions, tigers and bears, 4. 'CGV', 5. Strawberries, 6. A tree, 7. His lower lip, 8. 'I purple you', 9. *One Piece*, 10. 'Danger', 11. Jin, 12. Girls Generation, 13. Flower arranging, 14. *Celebrity Bromance*, 15. To rap a cypher.

ARMY

1. 'Adorable Representative M.C. for Youth', 2. Festa, 3. 'Go Go', 4. Bell, 5. 'Kim Namjoon! Kim Seokjin! Min Yoongi! Jung Hoseok! Park Jimin! Kim Taehyung! Jeon Jungkook! BTS!', 6. The member's solo works, 7. Justin Bieber, 8. July 2013, 9. Black Lives

Matter, 10. 'Flowers for ARMY', 11. 'I purple you', 12. Sowoozoo, 13. ARMY Bomb, 14. 'Young Forever', 15. MTV Video Awards.

SPORT AND GAMES

1. Suga, 2. Rock, paper, scissors, 3. Son Heung-min, 4. V, 5. Hanshin Tigers, 6. Wembley Stadium, 7. Jimin, 8. Jin, Jungkook and Jimin, 9. John Cena, 10. 4 × 100 metre relay, 11. *Overwatch*, 12. Traditional Korean wrestling, 13. J-Hope, 14. *League of Legends*, 15. Ice hockey.

COMPLETE THE TITLE

1. '... Heaven', 2. '... Fun', 3. '... a Strange City', 4. '... Girl', 5. '... Me', 6. '... Vu', 7. '... Bombs', 8. '... My Room', 9. '... Grey', 10. '... Bangtan', 11. '... Breaker', 12. '... Child', 13. '... Eternal', 14. '... Untold', 15. '... Go'.

ART AND LITERATURE

1. *Demian*, 2. The mountain of clothes, 3. *Kafka on the Shore*, 4. Jimin, 5. 'Serendipity', 6. *Starry Night*, 7. *Into the Magic Shop*, 8. 'Pied Piper', 9. Vante, 10. 'Blood Sweat & Tears', 11. J. M. W. Turner, 12. 'Spring Day', 13. Carl Jung, 14. *Catcher in the Rye*, 15. 'Daydream'.

SUGA BIAS

1. Basketball, 2. Beef, 3. Genius,
4. Sleeping, 5. Iced Americano,
6. Jin, 7. 2019 MAMAs, 8. Naruto,
9. Min Yoonji, 10. A snowman,
11. Orange, 12. 'Three dollars',
13. 'Tongue', 14. Sue him, 15. Hans
Zimmer.

GUESS THE SONG
FROM THE WORD

1. 'Dionysus', 2. 'Permission to
Dance', 3. 'ON', 4. 'IDOL', 5. 'MIC
Drop', 6. 'Go Go', 7. 'Dope',
8. 'Dynamite', 9. 'Anpanman',
10. 'Pied Piper', 11. 'Butterfly',
12. 'Hip Hop Phile', 13. 'Converse
High', 14. 'Butter', 15. 'Coffee'.

FEARS

1. I (elephants), 2. B (ghosts),
3. E (fireworks), 4. K (snakes),
5. A (butterflies), 6. G (mice), 7. C
(microwaves).

FESTA AND MUSTER

1. 'So 4 More', 2. 'Baepsae', 3. RM,
4. BT21 onesies, 5. 'Ddaeng',
6. 'Euphoria' and 'Daydream', 7. They
were recreations of classic group
photos, 8. 290, 9. The number of
hours BTS and ARMY had been
together, 10. RM and J-Hope,
11. ARMY Bombs, 12. 'Magic Shop',
13. The members had a water fight,

14. 'Daechwita' and 'Chicken Noodle
Soup', 15. 'microcosm' (it is the
Korean title of 'Mikrokosmos').

NAME THAT TOUR

1. The Wings Tour, 2. The Love
Yourself: Speak Yourself World
Tour, 3. The Red Bullet Tour, 4. The
Most Beautiful Moment in Life on
Stage Tour, 5. The Wake Up: Open
Your Eyes Tour, 6. The Map of the
Soul Tour, 7. The Love Yourself
World Tour.

BEHIND THE SCENES

1. Pdogg, 2. Supreme Boi, 3. Hiss
Noise, 4. Slow Rabbit, 5. El Capitxn,
6. They produce music videos, 7. Itzy,
8. Stray Kids, 9. Dior, 10. Sejin,
11. Keone Madrid, 12. Adora,
13. Ghost Band, 14. Main
choreographer, 15. Dave Stewart.

'LA, LA, LA' AND 'NA, NA, NA'

'Attack on Bangtan', 'Black Swan',
'DNA', 'Dynamite', 'Film Out', 'Filter',
'Fire', 'Home', 'Interlude: Wings',
'Ma City', 'Mikrokosmos', 'No More
Dream', 'ON', 'Permission to Dance',
'Spine Breaker', 'War of Hormone'.

V IN FOCUS

1. Kim Tae-hyung, 2. Daegu, 3. One
brother, one sister, both younger,
4. Farming, 5. *Hwarang: The Poet*

Warrior Youth, 6. Second youngest, 7. Jimin, 8. Wooga Squad, 9. 'I'm Good Boy', 10. TaeTae, 11. Saxophone, 12. 'It's no big deal', 13. Blue, 14. Louis Vuitton, 15. His skill on an arcade game on *Run BTS*.

US AND UK TV APPEARANCES

1. Fortnite, 2. 'Dynamite', 3. Ronan Keating of Boyzone, 4. 'Hey Jude', 5. Central Park, 6. 'I'll Be Missing You' by Faith Evans and Puff Daddy, 7. 2017 (AMAs), 8. *Friends*, 9. Emma Stone, 10. The Beatles, 11. 'Hook-up', 12. J-Hope, 13. Pyjamas and dressing gowns, 14. Grand Central Station, 15. Jimin.

INJURIES AND MISHAPS

1. V, 2. On his head, 3. Jin, 4. Futsal, 5. His ear, 6. Japan, 7. Neck and shoulder, 8. Jungkook, 9. Jimin, 10. RM, 11. Appendicitis, 12. Dancing close to fireworks, 13. His chair wasn't ready on time, 14. 'Fake Love', 15. Chile.

THE MOVIES

1. RM: *Eternal Sunshine of the Spotless Mind, Me Before You*, 2. Jin: *The Matrix, Pretty Woman*, 3. Suga: *Inception, Tazza*, 4. J-Hope: *Southpaw, A Star is Born*, 5. Jimin: *The Notebook, 3 Idiots*, 6. V: *About Time, Born to Be Blue*, 7. Jungkook: *The Hangover, Iron Man*.

BANGTAN PETS

1. Jimin, 2. 'Tonight', 3. Shih Tzu, 4. Yeontan, 5. RM ('RapMon' aka 'Moni'), 6. A poodle, 7. A cat, 8. Jungkook, 9. Jimin, 10. Sugar glider, 11. Soonshim, 12. 'Dope', 13. Jungkook, 14. Jimin, 14. 'Cloudie' (*gureum* is Korean for 'cloud'), 15. Jin.

RM BIAS

1. Pink, 2. Mad Scientist, 3. KAWS, 4. He lost an unreleased song while cleaning his PC, 5. 'Run', 6. Crabs, 7. Curly mohawk, 8. '… is still me', 9. 'Strange', 10. It's his IQ, 11. Ryan, 12. Blue, 13. 'Shut up, Malfoy', 14. Sailor Moon, 15. 'Namjooning'.

AWARDS

1. MMAs, 2. 'DNA', 3. H.E.R., 4. 'Boy Meets Evil', 5. Ariana Grande, 6. V, 7. 2016 (MMAs), 8. 2021 Grammys, 9. The UN, 10. Michael Jackson, 11. Jin, 12. Halsey, 13. Louis Vuitton, 14. Four (all of them!) in 2019, 15. GOT7.

WORDSEARCH

BTS LIVE

1. A record store (called Vinyl & Plastic), 2. The Red Bullet Tour, 3. A 'We love you' fanchant, 4. 'IDOL', 5. 'We are Bulletproof: the Eternal', 6. 'Baepsae', 7. 'Spring Day', 8. Seoul, 9. Suga and Jin, 10. 'DNA', 11. V, 12. 'Save Me', 13. Rock, paper, scissors, 14. '2! 3!', 15. 'Singularity'.

V SOLO

1. 'Stigma', 2. 'Christmas Tree', 3. A park, 4. V's grandmother, 5. *Itaewon Class*, 6. Sleep, 7. 'Inner Child', 8. 'Long Time No See', 9. 'Snow Flower', 10. In the street, 11. *About Time*, 12. 'Perfume dance', 13. Taking a photo, 14. Piano, 15. 'Blue & Grey'.

IN THE SOOP

1. J-Hope, 2. So he could make sashimi, 3. Jin, 4. 'Blue & Grey (English demo ver.)', 5. The *In the Soop* theme, 6. Jungkook and Jimin, 7. Avalon, 8. Bam (Jungkook's dog), 9. Trumpet, 10. Jimin, V and RM, 11. Tinkerbell, 12. Jimin, 13. Super Mario World, 14. 'IDOL', 15. Chef and waiter.

HOBBIES

1. Suga, 2. RM, 3. Jimin, 4. Jungkook, 5. J-Hope, 6. V, 7. Jin.

B-SIDES

1. 'Telepathy', 2. 'Sea', 3. 'Paradise', 4. The Chainsmokers, 5. 'We On', 6. Jungkook, 7. The group moving house, 8. 'Fly to My Room', 9. 'UGH!', 10. '2! 3!', 11. 'Jamais Vu', 12. '134340', 13. '00:00 (Zero O'Clock)', 14. BTS and their fans, 15. They sing in their regional dialects, aka *satoori*.

JIMIN BIAS

1. He kicks other members from behind, 2. 'Serendipity', 3. 'Practice', 4. Jimmy Fallon, 5. 'the red suit', 6. V, 7. You're late, 8. Black, 9. 'Nevermind', 10. Parkas, 11. 'Blood Sweat & Tears', 12. 'We are Bulletproof Pt. 2', 13. Bear figurines ('Winter Bear'), 14. SHINee's Taemin, 15. 'Prince Charming'.

YOU KNOW BTS MUSIC VIDEOS? PART 1

1. Chicago Bulls, 2. 'Faith',
3. Cleaning the boys' toilets,
4. White (with red and black edges),
5. Cuts his own hair, 6. At a petrol station, 7. Chicken, 8. Nirvana,
9. 'Bang', 10. Five members in black, two in white, 11. Bow and arrow,
12. German, 13. A motel,
14. Jungkook, 15. 'Yellow'.

SPOTIFY PLAYLISTS

1. J-Hope, 2. Suga, 3. Jimin,
4. Jungkook, 5. RM, 6. V, 7. Jin.

YOUTH ERA

1. *HYYH*, which stands for *hwa yang yeon hwa*, 2. Racing driver and private dectective, 3. RM, Suga, Jimin, 4. 'I Need U', 5. V, 6. J-Hope, Jimin and V, 7. MTV's *The Show Choice*, 8. A kiss, 9. 'Ma City', 10. A BTS media exhibition in Seoul, 11. 'Whalien 52', 12. A campervan/hot-air balloon adventure, 13. 'BOY MEETS', 14. 'Silver Spoon', 'Crow-Tit' or 'Try-Hard', 15. 'Dope'.

J-HOPE IN FOCUS

1. Jung Ho-seok, 2. 1994, 3. 'Hoya',
4. Gwangju, 5. JYP, 6. Literature,
7. Neuron, 8. Tennis, 9. Fashion (Mejiwoo and FUN THE MENTAL),
10. Jimin, 11. His father's video letter,
12. Hyungwon, 13. 'Boy in Luv', 14. Japan, 15. Sunshine.

CUT AND COLOUR

1. Suga, 2. Bright blue, 3. Platinum blond, 4. A bun, 5. V, 6. 'Butter',
7. A long blond high ponytail,
8. Love Yourself: Speak Yourself,
9. Jungkook, 10. Blond, 11. J-Hope,
12. AMAs, 13. An exposed forehead,
14. 'Dynamite', 15. All had black hair at the same time.

WHO SAID WHAT ABOUT WHOM?

1. Jimin on J-Hope, 2. Jimin on V,
3. Jungkook on RM, 4. Suga to Jungkook, 5. RM on Jin, 6. V on Jimin, 7. Jin on RM, 8. Suga on Jin,
9. Suga on J-Hope, 10. J-Hope on RM, 11. RM on J-Hope, 12. Jungkook on Jin, 13. Jin on Suga, 14. Jungkook on Jimin, 15. V on Jungkook.

JUNGKOOK SOLO

1. Justin Bieber, 2. 'Still with You',
3. 'Falling' by Harry Styles,
4. Sitting on a bed, 5. 'Stay Alive',
6. 'Euphoria', 7. He uploaded two versions, 8. V, 9. 'Paper Hearts',
10. 10,000, 11. 'Only Then',
12. When busking in Malta during *Bon Voyage* season 3, 13. Lady Jane,
14. 'Begin', 15. His father.

BANGTAN UNIVERSE

1. Songju, 2. Abraxas, 3. A theme park, 4. Smeraldo, 5. USA, 6. Namjoon, 7. His abusive father, 8. Fear, 9. Taehyung, 10. A Snickers bar, 11. Seokjin, 12. A motel, 13. Jungkook, 14. 'ON', 15. A white cat.

ICONIC MUSIC VIDEO MOMENTS

1. 'MIC Drop', 2. 'Boy With Luv', 3. 'Blood Sweat & Tears', 4. 'IDOL', 5. 'Permission to Dance', 6. 'Film Out', 7. 'Spring Day'.

BTS ON *THE LATE LATE SHOW WITH JAMES CORDEN*

1. 'You're joker guy', 2. 'Circles', 3. 'Papa Mochi', 4. Ashton Kutcher, 5. J-Hope, 6. Their own stage, 7. 'Flinch', 8. 'Covid-19 Pandemic', 9. Jimin, 10. 'Boy with Luv', 11. Dance class, 12. 'Black Swan', 13. 'Butter', 14. V, 15. 'hot water'.

WORLD RECORDS

1. Eight, 2. BangBangCon: the Live and Map of the Soul: ON:E, 3. Seven, 4. Replacing their own song ('Butter') at No. 1, 5. 50, 6. 'Begin', 7. 2019, 8. 'Daechwita', 9. Three, 10. Jimin, 11. Michael Jackson, 12. 'Dynamite', 13. V, 14. J-Hope, 15. 4 million.

MAP OF THE SOUL ERA

1. Grapes and strawberries, 2. 'Mikrokosmos', 3. 'Magic Shop', 4. Jimin, 5. RM, 6. London, 7. Five, 8. CONNECT, BTS, 9. *Singin' in the Rain*, 10. Central Park, New York, 11. 'Black Swan', 12. Sia, 13. Grand Central Station, New York, 14. '00:00 (Zero O'Clock)', 15. 'We are Bulletproof: the Eternal'.

JIN IN FOCUS

1. Kim Seok-jin, 2. 1992, 3. One older brother, 4. He ran away, 5. Play *League of Legends*, 6. Suga, 7. Japanese, 8. Australia, 9. *Eat Jin*, 10. Jin gave himself the nickname, 11. *MapleStory*, 12. Fishing, 13. Hearts, 14. 'It's Definitely You', 15. Third.

BTS ON THE BIG SCREEN

1. Pee on the couch, 2. A chocolate ball, 3. A pool party, 4. A banana, 5. Paris, 6. 'Fire', 7. The Grammy Museum, 8. 'Honsool', 9. Jungkook, 10. 'PERSONA', 11. New York City, 12. Wood art, 13. Jin, 14. Brushes his teeth, 15. Make eye contact with them.

JAPAN, PART 1

1. Jin, 2. 'Let Go', 3. 'Bird' 4. *Signal*, 5. 'For You', 6. June 2014, 7. Sushi, 8. KM-MARKIT, 9. Kobe, 10. *Wake*

Up, 11. Bōdan Shōnendan,
12. ... Open Your Eyes, 13. *BTS, the Best*, 14. 'I Like It', 15. Def Jam.

SUGA SOLO

1. 'Agust D' ('DT Suga' backwards, with DT for Daegu Town), 2. His piano, 3. 'Trivia: Seesaw', 4. RM, 5. 'What Do You Think?', 6. 'Suga's Interlude', 7. MAX, 8. 'Honsool', 9. 'Tony Montana', 10. 'It's a Man's Man's Man's World', 11. The king, 12. 'Song Request'. 13. A rap star, 14. 'Dear My Friend', 15. A sword.

COVER VERSIONS

1. 'Come Back Home', 2. 'Fix You', 3. Jungkook sang Charlie's part and Jimin sang Selena's, 4. 'Without a Heart', 5. Big Bang, 6. 'Born Singer', 7. V, 8. 'I'll Be Missing You', 9. 'Beautiful', 10. 'Santa Claus is Coming to Town', 11. 'Perfect Man', 12. Harry Styles, 13. RM, 14. 'Watermelon Sugar', 15. 'Rainism'.

JET-SETTING

1. His luggage, 2. At a petrol (gas) station, 3. Suga, 4. Diaries, 5. Sandboarding, 6. Helsinki, 7. Beer, 8. A stingray, 9. ARMY, 10. Suga to Jin, 11. All of them, 12. Maroon 5's 'Sunday Morning', 13. UNO, 14. Sun and moon, 15. South Korea.

JIMIN IN FOCUS

1. 'Fake Love', 2. Contemporary dance, 3. 13, 4. Magnate, 5. His height, 6. Park Ji-min, 7. A perfectionist, 8. 'Ddochi', 9. Because an injury prevented him from performing, 10. '*Ipdeok* (recruiting) Fairy', 11. Pale pink, 12. RM, 13. J-Hope, 14. Taekwondo, 15. Above his right eye.

COVER ART AND CONCEPT PHOTOS

1. Butterflies, 2. *The Most Beautiful Moment in Life: Young Forever*, 3. *Love Yourself: Tear*, 4. Pink, 5. *You Never Walk Alone*, 6. Four, 7. *Love Yourself: Answer*, 8. V, 9. 'Butter', 10. *Map of the Soul: 7*, 11. *Dark & Wild*, 12. 'Life Goes On', 13. J-Hope, 14. 'No School' (on *Skool Luv Affair*), 15. Seven.

FOOD

1. Sushi, 2. A sauce, 3. Chocolate bars, 4. Jin, 5. Dumplings, 6. Jungkook, 7. Banana, 8. Italian cooking, 9. Suga, 10. Churros, 11. Panda Express, 12. Steak and ratatouille, 13. Jimin, 14. Lamb skewer, 15. Onions.

ICONIC FASHION MOMENTS

1. Jungkook, 2. RM, 3. V, 4. Jimin, 5. Jin, 6. Suga, 7. J-Hope.

J-HOPE SOLO

1. 'Hixtape', 2. 'Blue Side (Outro)', 3. GOT7's Yugyeom, 4. *Twenty Thousand Leagues Under the Sea*, 5. 'Gangnam Style', 6. 'Hangsang', 7. 'Outro: Ego', 8. 'Piece Of Peace', 9. 'Don't Panic', 10. V, 11. Champagne, 12. '1Verse', 13. His mother, 14. 'Boy Meets Evil', 15. 'Trivia: Just Dance'.

BANGTAN BOMBS, PART 2

1. Suga, 2. J-Hope, 3. Jimin and J-Hope (especially J-Hope!), 4. Big Bang, 5. J-Hoooope!, 6. A thrift shop, 7. 'Danger', 8. 'Euphoria', 9. Jungkook and Jimin, 10. At a rollerskating rink, 11. BTS and ARMY, 12. Ice cream, 13. 'It's Definitely You', 14. Suga and RM, 15. Chicago.

LINES AND SUBUNITS

1. Jimin, V and Jungkook, 2. Suga and V, 3. Jin, Suga, J-Hope and RM, 4. Jimin and Jungkook, 5. Jin, RM and V, 6. RM, Suga and J-Hope, 7. V and Jimin, 8. Jin, V, Jungkook and Jimin, 9. RM and J-Hope, 10. J-Hope, Jungkook and Jimin, 11. Jin, V and Jungkook, 12. Suga and J-Hope, 13. Suga and Jimin, 14. Jin and J-Hope, 15. RM and Jimin.

YOU KNOW BTS MUSIC VIDEOS? PART 2

1. Mastermind World, 2. 'Save Me', 3. A giraffe, 4. Persona, 5. 'No More Dream', 6. The cape, 7. *The Maze Runner*, 8. Jimin, 9. Golden retriever, 10. Donuts and burgers, 11. Bonsai, 12. Suga, 13. Christie, 14. DJ Lafrique, 15. An hourglass.

KOREAN WORDS AND PHRASES

1. Happy, 2. Hello, 3. *Hwaiting!*, 4. Dialect, 5. A male friend or brother who is older than you, 6. *Selca*, 7. A friend, 8. The *maknae*, 9. Crow-tit, 10. *Aegyo*, 11. *Daesang*, 12. Make some noise, or literally, 'scream', 13. I love you, 14. 'A Poem for Small Things', 13. 'Awesome!'

J-HOPE BIAS

1. Zero, 2. Suga, 3. Lady Gaga, 4. Pre-debut, 5. Drake's #InMyFeelingsChallenge, 6. 'Awake', 7. 'Hug Me', 8. 'Hope on the Street', 9. Dior, 10. Hwagae, 11. 'A Brand New Day', 12. Becky G, 13. Purple, 14. Jin, 15. 'Dionysus'.

CRYPTIC CELEBRITY FANS

1. Ariana Grande, 2. John Cena, 3. Shawn Mendes, 4. Charli XCX, 5. Lizzo, 6. Tyra Banks, 7. Joe Jonas, 8. Camila Cabello, 9. Emma Stone, 10. Matthew McConaughey,

11. Whoopi Goldberg, 12. Stormzy,
13. Dylan O'Brien, 14. Maisie
Williams, 15. William Shatner.

BTS EXHIBITIONS

*The Most Beautiful Moment in Life
Pt. 2*, 2. Jungkook, V, RM, 3. Jimin,
4. Rabbit (or hare), 5. 'Euphoria',
6. Suga, 7. 'Five Always', 8. Five,
9. Berlin, 10. Hot-air balloon,
11. Antony Gormley, 12. BTS
choreography, 13. Map of the Soul
ON:E, 14. Futura, 15. Jimin.

BANGTAN BOYS IN LOVE

'Intro: Skool Luv Affair', 'Boy in Luv',
'Boy With Luv', 'Hip Hop Lover' (aka
'Hip Hop Phile'), 'First Love', 'Fake
Love', 'Love Maze', 'Love Is Not Over
(Full Length Edition)', 'Trivia: Love',
'Answer: Love Myself', 'Outro: Love
in Skool', 'Outro: Love Is Not Over'.

RUN BTS!

1. 'Dionysus' at the 2019 MMAs,
2. Zombies, 3. Jumping in the air,
4. Min Yoonji, 5. Jin, Jimin and
Jungkook, 6. Their mums, 7. Having
a short nap, 8. 'BTS Forever!',
9. Jimin, Jin, Jungkook and V,
10. J-Hope, 11. Suga and Jungkook,
12. Jimin – 'carbonara', 13. Jin (Team
100Jin vs Team 100Seok),
14. 'WoW', 15. Jungkook.

IN A WORD

'134340', 'Anpanman', 'Awake',
'Baepsae', 'Begin', 'Butter',
'Butterfly', 'Coffee', 'Danger',
'Dimple', 'Dionysus', 'Dis-ease',
'DNA', 'Dope', 'Dynamite',
'Euphoria', 'Filter', 'Fire', 'Heartbeat',
'Her', 'Home', 'IDOL', 'Interlude',
'Intro', 'Jump', 'Lie', 'Lights', 'Like',
'Lost', 'Mama', 'Mikrokosmos', 'N.O',
'ON', 'Outro', 'Paradise', 'Path'
(aka 'Road'), 'Rain', 'Reflection',
'Respect', 'Run', 'Sea', 'Serendipity',
'Singularity', 'Skit', 'Stay', 'Stigma',
'Tear', 'Telepathy', 'Tomorrow', 'Ugh!'

RM IN FOCUS

1. Kim Nam-joon, 2. 1994, 3. *Friends*,
4. New Zealand, 5. Jogger pants and
a wind chime, 6. Destruction,
7. Glam, 8. Jungkook and V,
9. Texas, 10. Jackson, 11. His nose,
12. Switzerland and Italy,
13. His passport, 14. Rollerskating,
15. Dance Monster.

FUNNY OUTFITS

1. Jin, 2. Suga, 3. J-Hope, 4. V,
5. Jimin, 6. RM, 7. Jungkook.

TRIVIA

1. Jimin and V, 2. Dream Challenge,
3. Jin, 4. 'Life Goes On', 5. Australia,
6. 'Partition' by Beyoncé, 7. Jin's
('Awake'), 8. Jungkook and V,

9. Jimin, 10. 'Closer', 11. Las Vegas,
12. Usher, 13. 'Super Tuna',
14. Martin Luther King Jr, 15. Jungkook.

JIMIN SOLO

1. 'Lie', 2. 'I Need U', 3. A genie,
4. V, 5. '24/7 = Heaven', 6. '95
Graduation', 7. 'Christmas Day',
8. RM, 9. *Love Yourself: Her*,
10. Red and purple, 11. 'Cake Waltz',
12. 2020, 13. 1 billion,
14. 'Serendipity', 15. An apple.

JAPAN, PART 2

1. Suga, 2. 23, 3. Suga and V, 4.
'Hold Me Tight' and 'Let Me Know',
5. Jungkook and Jimin,
6. RM and J-Hope, 7. 'Blood Sweat
& Tears', 8. *Youth*, 9. 'Baepsae'
('Silver Spoon'), 10. 'Stay Gold',
11. Jungkook, 12. 'Introduction:
Youth', 13. 'Crystal Snow', 14. His
toe, 15. In a bar.

FESTIVE BTS

1. 'A Typical Trainee's Christmas',
2. Christmas jumpers, 3. Justin
Bieber's 'Mistletoe', 4. V, 5. 'Snow
Flower', 6. 'Christmas Love', 7. Times
Square, 8. RM and Jungkook,
9. 'Awake', 10. 'Last Christmas',
11. Jungkook ('Oh Holy Night'),
12. V and Suga, 13. 'Run',
14. 'Santa Claus is Comin' to Town',
15. 'Snowman'.

LOVE YOURSELF ERA

1. 'DNA', 2. 'Airplane Pt. 2', 3. BT21
costumes, 4. 'Spring Day (Brit Rock
Remix)', 5. 'I'm Fine', 6. 'Best of Me',
7. Talks they had about disbanding,
8. Pluto, 9. A flower and Jin,
10. Flossing, 11. 'Pied Piper',
12. 'Answer: Love Myself',
13. 2018 BBMAs,
14. 'Ddaeng', 15. 'MIC Drop'.

BRAND PARTNERSHIPS AND ACCIDENTAL ENDORSEMENTS

1. Converse, 2. Seoul X BTS,
3. 'IONIQ: I'm on it', 4. Jessi, 5. Fila,
6. *Friends Must Fly Out*, 7. Gentle
Monster pink sunglasses, 8. Hyundai
Palisade, 9. Jungkook, 10. V and
Jimin, 11. Massage chair, 12. Mute
Boston bag, 13. McDonald's,
14. Louis Vuitton, 15. A mini-bag.

VARIETY AND REALITY SHOWS

1. *Rookie King*, 2. RM, 3. Jungkook,
4. Los Angeles, 5. *Knowing Bros*,
6. Cosmetics and skincare products,
7. *You Quiz on the Block*, 8. 'If You',
9. *Celebrity Bromance*, 10. *Running
Man*, 11. *I-Land*, 12. Jin, 13. *Under 19*,
14. V, Jimin and J-Hope, 15. *Go BTS!*.

SIGNATURE POSES

1. J-Hope, 2. Jin, 3. V, 4. RM,
5. Jimin, 6. Jungkook, 7. Suga.

WEBTOONS AND BT21

1. A cat, a monkey and a bunny,
2. *We On: Be the Shield*, 3. Axion (giant alien monsters), 4. Seok-jin,
5. Narcolepsy (sleep), 6. Koya, RJ, Shooky, Mang, Chimmy, Tata, Cooky and Van, 7. RM's (Koya),
8. Van, 9. Tata (V), 10. 'Anpanman',
11. Chimmy and RJ, 12. Sin-si,
13. *Beom* (the modern Korean word for tiger is *horangi*), 14. Jooan (V's character), 15. Jungkook.

JIN SOLO

1. 'Tonight', 2. *Love Yourself: Answer*,
3. His insecurities about being a musician, 4. 'In Front of the Post Office in Autumn', 5. Ra.D's 'Mom',
6. Piano, 7. 2015, 8. 'Awake', 9. 2016,
10. 'Abyss', 11. 'Spine Breaker',
12. 'Danger', 13. ARMY, 14. Jewels and gems, 15. A second verse.

COLLABORATIONS

1. G-Friend, 2. Jungkook and Jimin,
3. Billy Ray Cyrus, 4. 'Permission to Dance', 5. Megan Thee Stallion,
6. 'My Universe' (with Coldplay),
7. 'The Truth Untold', 8. 'IDOL',
9. 'All Night', 10. Jin, 11. 'ON (feat. Sia)', 12. Jungkook, Suga and J-Hope, 13. Friendship bracelets,
14. Block B, 15. Ed Sheeran.

INSTRUMENTS

1. Violin, 2. Drums, 3. Jin, 4. J-Hope,
5. Pink, 6. 'Black Swan', 7. Saxophone,
8. Flute, 9. On a recorder, with his nose, 10. Jungkook and Suga,
11. 'IDOL', 12. 'Love Yourself',
13. Ukelele, 14. Jin, 15. Trumpet.

NO. 1s

1. Eight, 2. *Love Yourself: Tear*,
3. Japan, 4. 'Blood Sweat & Tears',
5. 'Sweet Night', 6. 'Fire', 7. 'For You', 8. 'Yours' by Jin (*Jirisan* OST),
9. 'IDOL' (feat. Nicki Minaj),
10. *Map of the Soul: Persona*, 11. 35 months, 2PM's Junho, 12. Fifth,
13. *Map of the Soul: 7*, 14. 'Stay Alive', 15. 'Savage Love (Laxed – Siren Beat)'.

TRUE OR FALSE

1. True, 2. False, 3. True, 4. False,
5. True, 6. True, 7. False, 8. True,
9. True, 10. False, 11. True, 12. False,
13. True, 14. False, 15. False.

'DYNAMITE', *BE* AND 'BUTTER'

1. Blue (RM) and blond (V),
2. Jungkook, 3. UN General Assembly, 4. RM, Jin and Jungkook,
5. 'IDOL' and 'Mikrokosmos', 6. Best Pop Duo/Group Performance,
7. 'Make It Right', 8. Jimin, 9. 2020 AMAs, 10. 'Fly to My Room',
11. Their first US Billboard Hot 100 No. 1, 12. An animated block of

butter gradually melted, 13. Suga,
14. Jimin, 15. Los Angeles.

SET LIST
1. 'ON', 2. 'N.O', 3. 'We are
Bulletproof Pt. 2', 4. 'Intro: Persona',
5. 'Boy in Luv', 6. 'Dionysus',
7. 'Interlude: Shadow', 8. 'Black
Swan', 9. 'Ugh!', 10. '00:00 (Zero
O'Clock)', 11. 'My Time', 12. 'Filter',
13. 'Moon', 14. 'Inner Child',
15. 'Outro: Ego', 16. 'Boy With Luv',
17. 'DNA', 18. 'Dope', 19. 'No More
Dream', 20. 'Butterfly', 21. 'Run',
22. 'Dynamite', 23. 'We are
Bulletproof: the Eternal', 24. 'Spring
Day', 25. 'IDOL', 26. 'Dynamite',
27. 'We are Bulletproof: the Eternal'.

JUNGKOOK IN FOCUS
1. Jeon Jung-kook, 2. 1997, 3. Busan,
4. One older brother, 5. Laundry,
6. 20, 7. 'Muscle Pig', 8. His father,
9. 'My Time', 10. Billie Eilish's 'Bad
Guy', 11. The word 'truth', 12. Khaki,
13. 'GCF in Helsinki', 14. Eyebrow,
15. 'Rather be dead than cool'.

SOCIAL MEDIA
1. #StopAsianHate, 2. Red, 3. The
renegade, 4. 'Chicken Noodle Soup',
5. A kiss-face emoji and a selfie,
6. 'Army painted me', 7. Suga,
8. Fell off his chair and hurt his butt,
9. 'Bare Wit Me' by Teyana Taylor,

10. 2017, 11. V, 12. #Jimin,
13. @rkive, @jin, @agustd,
@uarmyhope, @j.m, @thv,
@abcdefghi__lmnopqrstuvwxyz,
14. 'Really hard', 15. Malibu, California.

BIG HIT
1. 'Hitman Bang' or 'Bang PD',
2. 2005, 3. g.o.d, , 4. A 'co-ed' vocal
group, with one female and two male
members, 5. GLAM, 6. Pdogg,
7. 2AM, 8. Homme, 9. Weverse,
10. GFriend, 11. Tomorrow X
Together, 12. RM, 13. HYBE
Corporation, 14. Enhypen, 15. Pledis.

V LIVE AND WEVERSE
1. In their dance studio, 2. Suga and
J-Hope, aka Sope, 3. DJ TaeTae FM,
4. *1Minute English*, 5. Jungkook,
6. ARMY Bomb light sticks, 7. Suga,
8. Jin, 9. A photo of Yeontan and the
username 'joo yoon tan', 10. Sitting
with his feet up, 11. Namjoon,
12. Tying his hair up, 13. *Hotteok*
(Korean pancakes), 14. A marriage
proposal to J-Hope, 15. Super Tuna
dance challenge.

PHOTO SECTION

P1

1. First BBMAs win for Top Social Artist, 2017
2. Addressing the UN as UNICEF ambassadors, 2018

P2

P3

1. Jungkook, 2. Jin, 3. RM, 4. V, 5. Suga, 6. Jimin, 7. J-Hope

P4–5

1. D – School Trilogy Era, 2. A – Love Yourself Era, 3. B – Map of the Soul Era, 4. C – Butter Era

P6

1. J-Hope   2. Suga   3. V   4. Jin

5. Jungkook   6. Jimin   7. RM

P7

1. BTS being appointed Special Presidential Envoys by President Moon Jae-in, 2021
2. Performing 'Butter' live at the Grammy Awards, 2022

P8

1. V, 2. Suga, 3. Jin, 4. Jungkook, 5. RM, 6. Jimin, 7. J-Hope

PHOTO CREDITS

Page 1: Jeffrey Mayer / WireImage / Getty Images (top); The Asahi Shimbun / The Asahi Shimbun via Getty Images (bottom)

Page 2: Axelle / Bauer-Griffin / FilmMagic / Getty Images

Page 3: Cindy Ord / WireImage / Getty Images (all)

Page 4: Jason LaVeris / FilmMagic / Getty Images (top); Astrid Stawiarz / Getty Images for Dick Clark Productions / Getty Images (bottom)

Page 5: Kevin Winter / Getty Images for MRC (top); The Chosunilbo JNS / Multi-Bits via Getty Images (bottom)

Page 6: The Chosunilbo JNS / Imazins via Getty Images (1); Han Myung-Gu / WireImage / Getty Images (2, 4, 6 & 7); Shutterstock (3); Cindy Ord / WireImage / Getty Images (5)

Page 7: Newscom / Alamy Stock Photo (top); Johnny Nunez / Getty Images for The Recording Academy (bottom)

Page 8: Steven Ferdman / Getty Images for ESB; illustrations from Shutterstock